The Dark Science of Psychological Warfare

How to Always Keep the Upper Hand On Anyone Psychologically

By Madison Taylor

D1446465

Table of Contents

Introduction

It is easy to batter someone with a knife, baseball bat, or other physical object. You can hurt someone physically quite easily. But then you usually face assault or murder charges. Also, someone could hurt you back in self-defense. Hurting someone physically involves many risks that are often not worth the little bit of satisfaction that you gain.

So, if you want to break someone, it is often better to use subtler methods. "What subtle method could I use?" you may ask, as you desperately search for a way to get back at your ex. Alternatively, you may not want to hurt anyone, but you really want to get your way in the world. People are always fighting you or disrespecting you and you want to finally win. How can you do this?

The answer is psychological warfare. With psychological warfare, you can use words, manipulation, and propaganda to break down your enemies and get them under your control. You can get people to do whatever you want by using certain psychological tricks and strategies upon them. You do not require any strength or any allies to make this work to your favor. The beauty of psychological warfare is that you can do it entirely on your own, using your own smarts and special faculties.

Psychological warfare is no joke. You can easily batter someone mentally until they are completely broken inside. You can gain great control over people using the methods of psychological warfare. And the best part? You will not face jail time or the risk of physical harm. There are no laws against psychological warfare and no one will even suspect you of doing anything wrong. That is, if you do psychological warfare right.

You do not have to worry about doing it right. This book will teach you everything you need to know. In these pages, you will learn the fine details of subtly and successfully taking control of someone's mind. Using the most underhanded mental techniques, you can wreak havoc on someone's mind. You are basically declaring war on someone mentally, and ensuring your chances of winning.

With psychological warfare, you are using the rules of human psychology to your advantage. As a result, you are almost guaranteed success. People respond to certain hints and tricks the same, and employing them will result in success for you. You are sure to win a war with psychology rather than with brute force.

Using psychological warfare also calls for you to be very calculating and cunning. You can spring attacks on people that they are simply not prepared for. People are not able to prepare for psychological attacks. You have the element of surprise to your advantage.

Psychological warfare is far sneakier than you can imagine. Your subject and his friends and family may sense that something is wrong, but they will not be able to prove you guilty of any wrongdoing. You will find that mental control is far tighter than physical control, and you can truly decimate your victim. Cleanly and ruthlessly, you can finish a war with someone and emerge the victor. You can subdue people without having to put up a strenuous fight. Then you have control, and you are unstoppable.

When war rages between countries or governments, the physical side is very obvious. People see the bombings and fatalities and body counts. What they fail to notice is the psychological side of war. Enemies can be won over or subdued using very clever and subtle tricks, such as flyers spreading propaganda messages that turn civilians against their governments. Even soldiers giving out candy to young children in villages in enemy countries are employing a form of psychological warfare. Psychological warfare is what often silently wins the war. The best part is that no one notices. It is so sneaky and covert because it is entirely mental.

The United States is especially adroit at psychological warfare. There is a reason that the United States is one of the most powerful countries in the world. Without even going to war all the time, the United States is able to keep control over many countries using propaganda and trade. If you learn from the United States government, you can set yourself up for success in using covert psychological operations to win all of your personal battles. People will have no clue what you are doing as you gain control over their minds and even their hearts. In the end, you will win, without even going to war. And your victims will have no idea what just happened to them. They will essentially give you control and submit to you of their own volition.

Doesn't that sound amazing to have that kind of power? It is amazing. But the content of this book is not to be taken lightly. This is your one and only warning. If you use these methods, you can get some extremely fast and certain results. You can take control of someone, and you can break someone. Use this book on your enemies, not on your friends.

Many of the methods contained in this book were perfected by the US government and other entities, such as the KGB. They are tried and true. This makes them all the more dangerous. Your enemies should be really scared right now, because you are learning the very best weapon that exists.

Chapter 1: What is Psychological Warfare?

What Is It?

Psychological warfare is the more mental side of war. It is very insidious, both because of its high level of power, and because of its subtlety. Many people do not realize that they have been victims of psychological wars until they learn the signs and techniques. Psychological warfare involves using subtle methods to influence or alter someone's beliefs, feelings, and behavior, thus gaining control over someone from a distance. When you are in control of a person's mental and physical processes, you have tremendous power over the person. You can influence someone to do whatever suits your needs.

Psychological warfare uses a large variety of techniques to subdue the enemy. You can use light and sound to cause subliminal effects on your enemy's mind. You can use propaganda, rumors, and other forms of public communication to influence someone's decisions. You can ruin a person's reputation and their confidence. Through a variety of physical, mental, and emotional means, you can gain control over someone and ruin someone's life. The fine techniques of psychological warfare are covered in more detail in later chapters.

Psychological warfare is typically far more effective than any other form of attack. Not only are you able to remain totally undetected, but you can also cause true harm. There are no laws against psychological warfare.

There are other names for psychological warfare. These include PSYOP (Psychological Operations), heart and mind, propaganda, political warfare, and MISO (Military Information Support Operations). These names give you a hint that psychological warfare is a favorite operation employed by the military. Governments use psychological warfare in war and intelligence because it is very effective and very covert.

Real Life Applications

There are four common uses for psychological warfare. First, this can be used to influence foreign people and governments to take stances that is friendly to the invading government. For instance, the United States could convince the people of an African nation to hate their own government. The people start a revolution, which breaks down the government. The United States can then easily invade the country, using the guise that they are providing "aid" and taking advantage of the fact that the military is too preoccupied with the revolution to stave off the invasion.

Second, psychological warfare involves strategic spats of terror to control a population. Acts of random violence, espionage, and other methods put people in a constant state of anxiety and fear. People are thus more likely to accept anything in order to gain some sort of relief. A government or dictator can easily take advantage of a situation where people are terrified, just by promising people safety.

Third, brainwashing, hypnosis, and other forms of mind control and manipulation are employed to change others' personalities and viewpoints. People become tools and are changed or altered against their own wills. The government and the media can work together to change the general opinions of its people.

Finally, psychological warfare can be used to mold the general attitudes of entire populations. A classic example of this is how American people were molded to hate terrorists, without entirely understanding just who or what the enemy was. What exactly are terrorists? Are they Muslim extremists, or do they include other groups of people? Governments use this modeling to drive public opinion and gain the support needed for war. Governments can influence its own people to support a cause, when the government really has a secret agenda.

Referring to the terrorist example, it is theorized that the American hatred of the terrorist was used by the US government to garner public support for an oil war in the Middle East. While this is certainly a matter of opinion, it is an example of how a government can earn its people's support for a public agenda, when really it has an entirely different, secret reason for wanting war.

All of these methods are used by governments in real life. However, you can adapt them for personal use. People can and do adapt government psychological warfare methods all the time for their own personal agendas.

You can use troublemaking and instigating tactics to turn people against each other or their idols. You can undo their personal beliefs. By disabling the social supports and belief systems of people, you can disable everything that gives them strength. People will fall into chaos without the frameworks that they have created for their own minds.

You can use terror to subdue people. When your enemies are scared, you have the ultimate power. You can offer them relief if they do something for you, or you can coerce them with threats. Fear is a powerful motivator.

You can also change peoples' personalities to suit your desires. You can brainwash people to become automatons at your mercy. Over time, you can get them to abandon beliefs and values that go against your personal ends. In the end, you will have the ultimate emotional and mental slave.

Covertly, you can get people to root for causes and unintentionally serve secret agendas that you have. For instance, you can get people to donate to your charity by convincing them that you support a cause that they are passionate about. What people don't know is that your charity is actually set up in order to grant tax benefits for a politician.

Media and news companies are often guilty of employing psychological warfare.

Presidential campaign coverage is an example of how media outlets try to use psychological warfare techniques, such as propaganda, to influence people to vote for a certain candidate. Tom Brokaw is one news anchor who was accused of subliminally influencing people to vote for certain Republican candidates every year. Without intending to influence people, Brokaw would dedicate a certain enthusiasm to the candidates he liked, unintentionally spinning these candidates in a more appealing light. His viewers, who were already primarily Republican, were thus even more influence to vote for these candidates after watching his broadcasts.

Most people are still unaware of the nuances of psychological warfare. That is partly what makes it so useful. It is largely covert, so enemies are caught unaware and unprepared. They do not even know that their government or another individual is attacking them. Rather, people only feel that they are being goaded into doing what is right. They become excited and loyal to causes without understanding the hidden motives that lie behind these causes. The deliberate misdirection of people is a clever and almost foolproof way to influence people psychologically to serve your own personal ends.

The government uses psychological warfare to gain control over its citizens and other countries' citizens. But you can use psychological warfare to gain control over the people in your life. The home use of psychological warfare is similar to the military's use of it, but your purpose is probably either to get your way or to hurt someone close to you. You can adapt the methods employed by the government to make psychological warfare work for you in a personal setting.

There are many personal benefits to psychological warfare. Using the second guessing, manipulation, deception, persuasion, and torture advice contained in this book, you can achieve whatever you want. You can psychologically hurt people until they are no longer threats to you. You can manipulate and persuade people to give you whatever you want. You can even make people want to date you or befriend you because of your power over them. People will become your enemies or your allies, and everyone will fear you and respect your wishes.

Read on to find out the ways to adapt government methods in order to use psychological warfare to your personal advantage.

The History of Psychological Warfare

It is hard to cite the exact history of psychological warfare since it has been employed by governments and individuals throughout history. The psychological side of war is something that many people are unaware of, but it has always existed. It is believed to be an aspect in every conflict since the beginning of conflict. Since the human race is prone to conflict and violence, this means that the use of this kind of warfare is very ancient indeed.

Humans have long understood the power of psychological warfare and have found it to be a useful partner with physical fighting.

British military analyst and historian J.F.C. Fuller first coined the term "psychological warfare" in 1920. But the actual concept of psychological warfare, and the term itself, did not come into public popularity until the 1950s. World War II's psychological tactics helped spawn this public obsession with the topic. Exactly what psychological warfare entailed was hardly clear, however. Even today, it is not a totally clear or well-known topic. Some people attribute the methods of psychological warfare entirely to the military and actual war, while others attribute it to emotional abuse and tactics that you can use personally. The latter definition is the one that we are choosing to use in this book.

Psychological warfare is so old that it is impossible to determine who invented it. Humanity as a whole can reasonably be credited with this method, since governments of all cultures have employed it throughout history. Sun Tzu's *The Art of War* is an ancient text that highlights many psychological warfare tactics that the Chinese military employed in the 500 BCs and thereabouts.

Examples of psychological warfare are increasingly present today with our global ease of access to media. The entire world population has better access to information regarding to what is going on throughout the globe. It is no longer difficult to find out many different sides on important global issues. Even the mainstream media no longer has control of how people receive the news, with the advent of new media sites such as WikiLeaks. Psychological aspects of war, propaganda, and secret government agendas are gaining increasing public awareness.

While World War II certainly popularized this concept among the public throngs, the Cold War is the best example of psychological warfare at work available. Studying the Cold War is practically like reading a manual on how to perform psychological warfare. The United States and Soviet Union both took psychological warfare, as well as economic warfare, to the next level in their tense race for dominance in the 1950s and 1960s.

The main psychological technique that both sides employed in the Cold War was fear. People lived in terror of an impending nuclear attack. Bomb shelters and underground hideouts where built all over the United States and the Soviet Union in preparation. Chilling cartoons made during this time reflected the tense emotional atmosphere of the era.

The Soviet Union and United States both were notorious for broadcasting white noise. Eavesdroppers mistook the white noise for encryption and dedicated much time and money to decrypting broadcasts for naught. They also recruited spies who looked so innocent that doubt was then formed for all other innocent-looking individuals and paranoia for spies ran high. Hypnosis, torture, and other methods were frequently and mercilessly used on captured spies in an effort to get as many names of other spies as possible. Secret agents abounded, raising the paranoia and frustration of secrecy. Largely the war was fought with emotions and no one side ever knew what the other was really up to.

In the Gulf War and the War against Terrorism, psychological warfare played a large role. Pamphlets meant to strike fear in the hearts of civilians were distributed to encourage people to desert their countries or turn against their governments. Rumors and stories were spread to stir up hatred, fear, and terror. Rape and strategic bombings were often used to break the enemy's will down. Finally, US troops were known to play agitating broadcasts that encouraged enemies in hiding to come out and engage in fighting. The emotions of fear and despair and agitation were used liberally to hurt the Middle Eastern enemies.

Nowadays, the global access to information through the Internet, TV, and radio has made psychological warfare easier to use than ever before. You have many media tools at your advantage to begin a psychological war, whether your war is on a personal or political plane. So many people have access to the media and they blindly absorb its information without asking questions. They will believe propaganda and lies without seeking additional evidence. Therefore, you can easily use subliminal cues and blatant lies to convince others to follow your agenda.

The media is adept at revealing a carefully fabricated reality to viewers. Most people accept that what they see on the news is true. They are not aware that they are being manipulated by higher powers that they are not even aware of. For instance, Baghdad Bob was an Iraqi diplomat who gave daily news briefings on the state of the war. He lied blatantly to the Iraqi people, claiming that they were winning at the war and that Baghdad was safe from nuclear attack. Most people in his country and the surrounding Middle Eastern nations saw him speaking on TV and believed him. The Baghdad bombings came as a shock to most people as a result.

The wildfire power of Internet hoaxes is a further example of how people will believe anything that they see in the media that is presented to them. Certain hoaxes, such as the hoax that people accidentally eat eight spiders a year in their sleep, spread across the Internet and are accepted by Internet users as fact. Many people approach media, even on the Internet, without skepticism.

It is possible to manipulate and control people through news outlets and other media, since people believe what they are told. Media anchors have established a level of authority. Therefore, they exert that authority and most people accept what they say as truth. But in reality, the media is perfectly capable of, and well-known for, skewing the news certain ways and selecting what they show people to create a carefully designed picture of reality that is not always accurate. People can be influenced and driven to certain actions and emotions based on what they are shown. People may be influenced to vote for a certain political candidate, for instance, or they may be lulled into a false sense of security about their country's success in a war.

In addition, the Internet is a great way to smear someone's reputation, a psychological warfare tactic that we shall cover in more detail later. People on the Internet are strangers so their social media and business pages are their first impressions. If they make a bad first impression with their online presence, this can be very detrimental to them in business and in their personal lives. You can post embarrassing photos, negative reviews, and misinformation to sabotage someone's online reputation. This can adversely affect someone's business and job prospects. Also known as cyberbullying, the

Internet is a rich playground in which you can mold someone's reputation into something ugly. It is also a place where you can post things that can very much hurt a person's feelings.

Cyber attacks and hacking are also now possible. You can obtain sensitive and embarrassing information about someone. The Internet makes it easy to spy on people and glean their personal information and details. You can even read their "private" emails and chat conversations with surprising ease. You can learn so much about them that you can stalk them without much effort. By dropping hints or taking control of a person's computer, you can make them feel like they are going crazy.

Today's Information Age is undoubtedly the best and easiest time to wreak havoc on someone or on the world in general. Take advantage of the plethora of technology available to you to infiltrate the media or someone's life.

Proof that Psychological Warfare Works

The very timelessness of psychological warfare indicates its advantageous application. The various governments that have used psychological warfare throughout time prove that it really works. Governments would not rely so heavily on psychological warfare if it was not so fabulously successful. Sun Tzu's work *The Art of War* is commonly celebrated as a surefire guide on how to win wars.

The recent Iraqi war is one example where psychological warfare has effectively worked. Using various methods, the US government has been able to use propaganda to ignite fear and hatred in both the US and Islamic countries. Meanwhile, Islamic terrorists have effectively created terror in the US, Israel, France, and other countries through selective terror attacks and suicide bombings. Now all countries live in fear of attacks. This is part of the psychological torture that terrorist organizations desire.

However, you have probably witnessed psychological warfare firsthand in your personal life. Think of someone in your office or family who always is able to get you to do exactly what he or she wants. This person is probably great at saying things to you that strike you with fear or make you doubt yourself. You may have neighbors that try to ruin your daily life with torturous actions, and you are afraid to complain because they are intimidating. You may have even been bullied in school by someone who was able to make you feel awful about yourself and scared all of the time. People who are able to change your actions and your emotions through non-physical means are using psychological torture on you. They have been able to exert a large amount of control over you and take charge of your life by manipulating your actions.

You can see from these people that psychological warfare really works. But now that you are convinced about its efficacy, you probably wonder how you can possibly use it yourself. The methods that other people use to gain psychological control may seem dauntingly complex. Often, their methods are too subtle to actually study. That is all right, because this book will teach you everything you need to know.

In about 1513, an Italian aristocrat and diplomat named Niccolo Machiavelli wrote *The Prince*. This book is like a special guide for how one can be calculating, manipulative, and cunning in order to run a country and thus control people. Sun Tzu's *Art of War* is another guide. Both of these texts are very old and indicate the timeless reverence that people have held for psychological warfare. We will refer to these texts when teaching you about efficient and useful applications and techniques for psychological warfare.

Chapter 2: How to Decimate Your Opponent

In this chapter, tried and true methods of psychological warfare will be covered in detail. These are the tips that will actually decimate your opponent. They are not to be used lightly because of their very real and successful applications in psychological warfare.

Primary Targets

When you are employing psychological warfare, there are four targets that you must keep in mind. You must focus on these targets to enjoy success. Becoming distracted from these targets makes you vulnerable to losing the control that psychological warfare grants you.

The Mind

You want to focus on gaining control over someone's mind. You must view the mind as your target, rather than a person. A person's mind is the key to his overall sanctity. If you target his mind, you can thus gain complete control over the person.

It is easiest to gain control over the mind through emotions. Thoughts are hard to control, but if you control the emotions that lead to someone's thoughts, you can gain total thought control. The secret to emotional control is to play with someone's emotions through fear, guilt, and obligation. These three emotions are the key emotions that allow you control over someone's thoughts and actions.

Fear is the best motivator in the world. By striking fear in someone, you can greatly influence his actions. You can convince him to act in certain ways to avoid your threats. You can also get him to feel uncomfortable and lower the quality of his life. Some subtle ways to cause fear in people involve making someone doubt himself or his sanity, making someone fear for his loved ones, and making someone fear that he will become hated. Lowering someone's self-esteem is another significant way to strike fear in him.

He will become worried that he is unlovable, which is definitely one of the worst feelings that a human being can experience. Humans are herd animals and they require love and care.

Guilt also drives people to act. Guilt is such an uncomfortable emotion that people will do amazing things to escape it. You can make people feel guilty, even for transgressions that they have not committed, by pouting or showing them how hurt you are. To escape the feeling of guilt, people will go to great lengths to absolve their guilt. You can take advantage of someone's guilt to get them to do you favors.

Obligation is a good way to make people do what you want. You can make people feel obligated to do things for you by doing them favors. The more favors you do, the more obligated you can make people. A person who feels like he is in your debt will go to great lengths to satisfy that debt. This plays on the concept of reciprocity, where people exchange a favor for a favor, an eye for an eye.

These three emotions form the acronym FOG. FOG is an apt acronym, for it describes a sort of fog that you can pull over a victim's mind. With FOG, you can drive someone to act in certain ways. You do not have to make it apparent that you are using FOG. FOG works because people will play right into it themselves. FOG works on natural human emotions.

Peace

By targeting someone's peace, you can make him miserable. People rely on their peace and cherish it. You can ruin someone's peace in a variety of ways. Just using noise disturbances can disrupt the peace of your neighbors. Creating uncomfortable vibes for people in social settings can also disrupt peace. People will strive to retain their peace and will do anything to avoid disruption.

Reputation

Most people are very protective of their reputations. A person's reputation is how he is known and viewed by others. A person can lose friends and loved ones, and even business opportunities, if he has a bad reputation. Targeting someone's reputation can make you the master of someone's success. You can tear away his friends, family, and business relations by hurting his reputation. Launching an attack on someone's reputation is punishable by law as libel or slander. However, you can circumvent this by either being discreet in your slander, or by spreading the truth. Most people have very real dirt in their pasts. By exposing this dirt, you are legally smearing someone's reputation and lowering him in the eyes of his peers.

Idols

People have to have an idol to look up to. Idols can include religious figures such as saints, real people such as celebrities or political leaders, and fake figures such as fashion brands. People look to their idols for leadership and security. Disabling someone's idol can make someone feel lost and confused and even disillusioned with life. You can easily tear down someone's idol by brainwashing him to turn against his idols. You can also destroy an idol's reputation so that people lose faith in him. This happened with OJ Simpson and with Michael Vick.

The Prince

Niccolo Machiavelli's novel *The Prince* is an excellent diatribe on the ways that you can take control of other people. Often, Machiavelli's methods involve manipulation, cunning, and deceit. There is little physical action required in psychological warfare. From Machiavelli's ideas arose the concept of "Machiavellianism," which entails the use of covert tactics to achieve personal gain. The feelings and pride of other people are unimportant when using Machiavellianism to get your way. You are focused entirely on your end goal. The ends justify the means, in your eyes. This is the key to psychological warfare.

When using Machiavellian thought, you are assuming a position of leadership. You need to view yourself as a leader to gain control of others. Unapologetically take control of situations and then other people will be at your mercy. This is how you can begin to leverage psychological warfare on others.

Do not Worry about the Opinions of your Subordinates

You do not have to give anyone the time of day. The opinions of other people are not important. Do not make decisions based on the consensus of others, or you will appear weak. Instead, make decisions yourself and ignore the input of others. You will appear stronger and you will take a great deal of power into your own hands by not letting other people govern you with their ideas and opinions.

Use your Power

If you have power, don't be afraid to use it. Hesitating or stalling makes you look weak. It can leach away your power very quickly. You must be willing to take charge and start using your power the minute you get it. Command respect and let people know that you will not be beaten down. Make decisions quickly and use your authority the minute you get it.

Get your Hands Dirty

When you are faced with a situation that you know nothing about, do not betray your innocence. A lack of knowledge will only make you seem weak and make you lose respect. Instead, get your hands dirty without asking any questions or wasting any time. You will learn quickly as you go along. In other words, "just wing it."

Befriend Weaker People and Avoid Stronger Ones

The weaker people in life seek friendship. Actually, they do not seek it, they desperately need it. By taking advantage of this desperation, you can make weaker people flock around you.

They will be willing to subordinate themselves to you because you offer them the strength that they do not have. You can make the weak people in life turn to you as a leader and then they will become loyal companions to you.

Defend what is Truly Important to You

Know what is important and defend that. Let go of the lesser things. You must choose your battles. Life presents us with many battles, and some of them are simply wastes of time. Instead of expending your energy fighting unimportant battles, conserve your strength for big battles that truly matter. That way, you can defend what is important to you and you can crush other people by bringing in your biggest, best warfare.

Present Yourself Well

Presentation is everything. By presenting yourself as a respectable authority figure, people are more likely to trust you and respect you. Present yourself like you are always right, you are strong, and you are confident. Have a great posture, dress well, and take pride in your appearance. Talk when you want to talk and never stop talking for someone else; no one is allowed to talk over you. Give firm handshakes and maintain unwavering eye contact. All of these things send a message that you are not someone to mess with. You need to project confidence and authority if you want to be respected in this world.

Take on Risk

Show the world that you are the boss by fearlessly doing things, without hesitating at the possibility of risk. Risk is inevitable. Do not let it stop you or make you think twice. If you do, you give risk power over you, and you appear weak in the eyes of your peers. Approach risk as a problem that you can solve, not something that strikes fear in you.

As a good leader, you want to encourage others to approach risk as a mere problem to solve, as well. Lead people fearlessly through risk. This will make you a respectable leader.

Don't Trust Luck

Luck is not real. It is a phantom illusion. When you trust luck, you give other people and other things power over you. Do not trust in something that is so beyond your control. Take control yourself and make the changes or take the chances that you want. Only you can bring yourself a positive outcome, not luck.

Be the Best or Copy the Best

You need to appear to be the best to others to earn their trust, loyalty, and respect. People will want to do anything for you if you are the best. If you do not know how to be the best at what you do, then copy other people who have it figured out. Copy great successful leaders in your field of work, or crime novel villains who easily seduce and manipulate people around you.

Do Not Be Afraid to Bend the Laws

You can bend or even break the laws that rule society, social interaction, and conversation. By doing so, you show the world that you are your own boss. No one can control you, not even the authorities, real or imagined by society. You set your own rules and play by your own rules. Other people will actually admire this and they will strive to play by your rule book in order to earn your favor.

Use the Milton Model

The Milton Model is a form of neuro-linguistic programming, also known as NLP. NLP calls for modeling to make people act in certain ways. The Milton Model is an NLP model where you speak in vague terms so that people project what they want onto your words. Basically, you leave yourself open to interpretation. This way, people cannot blame you for their decisions. You can also influence people, without directly telling them to do anything.

You can get people to agree with anything you say by using the Milton Model. People will put their own interpretation onto your words, and then they will say yes. They do not realize what they are really getting themselves into.

Meta Modeling

Again, using NLP is helpful in creating models for how people should behave. You can influence how people behave by dissecting their speech. People often say things out of habit. They will use words like "everyone," "never," and "always." Rarely are these terms accurate. If you challenge it when people use these terms, you can make people start to question what they really mean. You can gain great control over people by making them constantly doubt what they are saying. You can make people start to introspect themselves in an effort to become more pleasing to you.

For instance, if someone says, "Everyone loves me!" you can disable his grandiose confidence by asking, "Are you sure everyone does?" or "What is love by your definition?" With these questions, you make someone start to doubt his confidence that everyone loves him. He will begin to watch his words around you, for fear that you will point out how he is wrong.

Do not allow exaggeration or any other form of grandiose self-expression. Gain control over people by analyzing and questioning everything they say, in order to make them question themselves. You are both gaining control and disabling others' self-esteem.

Use Mirroring

You can make people feel close to you if you subtly mimic their body language and movements. You do not want to do this obviously, as it will irritate people. But if you subtly imitate their motions after a brief two-second pause, you will make people feel that you like them. People will thus strive to please you, to keep your affection.

One of the easiest ways to employ mirroring is to lean toward someone while they are talking to you. Lean in toward them at the same exact angle that they are leaning toward you. This builds a sort of silent, subconscious rapport between you two.

Representational Systems

Some people are visually inclined. They will say things like, "See what I mean?" Other people are more audio inclined and will say, "Do you hear what I'm saying?" Yet others may be more tactile and will say, "Do you feel what I'm saying?" Listen to these cues for what representational, or sensory, system people prefer. Then talk to them using their preferred system. This will make people feel like they have a rapport with you, and they will strive to please you more.

Sun Tzu's Thirty-Six Strategies

In the following pages are thirty-six psychological warfare strategies that we will cover in detail. This is the meat of the subject; this section will teach you how to actively engage in psychological warfare. While these methods are predominantly used by the military, I have offered some adaptations for personal use. You can adapt any of these military methods as you see fit for your own war.

These techniques were collected and described in detail in a special Chinese military text by Sun Tzu from the Chinese Warring States Era, which fell between 403 and 221 BC. The exact age of this text is unknown, but its purpose is clear: to decimate the enemy. Despite its age, this ancient text is still relevant today for its ruthlessness and brutality. These methods were used by Chinese military in ancient history, and now they are still used today. Many of these techniques seem almost intuitive because they have become such a deep and accepted part of warfare for the entire human race. The thirty-six methods outlined in this text have only one purpose, and that is to break the enemy down completely. The success of these methods is doubtless, considering their timelessness.

Understanding that these methods come from a Chinese text is necessary to understand the language. Often, a Chinese metaphor is used to help convey the subject matter.

Deceive the Sky to Cross the Ocean

It is better to be obvious than sneaky. If you sneak around, hiding in the shadows, you will only look like you are up to no good. It will draw attention to you. If you act in an obvious way, it appears that you are being honest and upfront. People will not suspect you of any wrongdoing at all.

Besiege Wei to Seize Zhao

You do not have to attack your enemy directly to hurt him. Sometimes, attacking what he cherishes is far better. You can hurt someone and make life unbearable for him by destroying what he loves best. Almost everyone has a weakness: a spouse, a lover, children, a good friend, a pet, a favorite place, home.

This wisdom comes from a part of Chinese history, when the state of Wei attacked the state of Zhao. The state of Qi was not strong enough to attack Wei's army head-on, so instead Qi besieged its capital city.

Kill with a Borrowed Knife

You cannot fight every battle by yourself. Sometimes, tricking or getting someone to fight for you is effective. You don't have to do the dirty work and someone else can take the fall for your actions. Bribery, threats, and extortion are ways to get other people to fight your enemies for you. Use people like judges, the mailman, and even the banker to turn against your enemy. These ordinary people are great tools for making life very difficult for him.

This is especially useful when you are working to drive someone crazy. You can use the help of others to create a fake reality that jars with your victim's sense of what is real. The use of common people, such as grocery store clerks, can help cement the fake reality and make your victim begin doubting his sanity.

Substitute Leisure for Labor

It pays to relax and exist in leisure. This may seem like a waste of time, but really it is a great way to gather your faculties together for battle. While your enemy runs around wasting energy and time trying to attack you, you conserve your energy. Then, when your enemy is exhausted, you can easily strike.

Take your time and carefully plan your attack without letting your enemy know what you are thinking. The more prepared you are, the better your chances of winning.

Make Noise in the East, then Attack from the West

Distract your enemy with some sort of feint so that you can perform a different form of attack and catch him off guard. Start to make an obvious move that he might expect you to make, then turn around and make a move that he did not expect at all.

For instance, he might expect you to try to steal his girlfriend to hurt him. Make a move on his girlfriend by flirting with her. He will begin focusing on protecting her from your advances and securing his relationship, and his guard will be down in all other directions. Then secretly go and expose that he has been cheating on his girlfriend. You will destroy his relationship and his reputation without actually stealing his girlfriend.

Create Something from Nothing

Using the concept of making feints, you can scare your enemy by performing one feint. Then perform the same feint again. He will probably react to the first two feints, but not the third. He will think that you are bluffing again. Thus, when you make this feint, it actually is not a feint. It is the real attack.

Back to our above example, the third time you go for his girlfriend should be the time that you actually steal her. He will be caught unaware and he will be surprised that your third feint was the actual attack.

Loot a House on Fire

When someone is weak, he cannot fend you off. That is when you can successfully attack him and destroy him. Wait until your victim is broken by a life event, such as a death in the family or financial ruin. When his self-esteem is lowest and his resources and friends are fewest, you have the best chance of truly destroying him. He will not have his normal defenses up.

It is best to choose victims that are the most vulnerable. When you pick a victim who is strong, you will likely get a good fight. Vulnerable people have holes in their armor that you can easily find and pierce with a metaphorical sword.

Sneak through the Passage of Chencang

First, attack your enemy head-on with your best and main force. Then, use a second, more sinister attack to blindside him. Your enemy will not be able to cope with two separate attacks. He will split his thought and resources to battle the two attacks simultaneously, becoming disoriented and confused. He cannot win if he is all over the place fighting you.

You can employ this strategy in real life by yourself or with the help of another person. First, launch an attack on someone's reputation. As he desperately scrambles to clean up the damage and dispel the rumors that you have created about him, he will not be prepared for when a friend of yours begins to leak negative information about him to the public. Now he will be going crazy, trying to run damage control. He will probably become so confused and desperate that he will utter some sort of blunder that will confirm the rumors that you have started about him. People will come to distrust him and he cannot fix the damage.

This term also refers to a piece of Chinese military history. The general Liu Bang pretended to be fixing the roads so that his army could move into Guanzhong to attack Xiang Lu. Xiang Lu developed a false sense of security, believing that it would take Liu Bang forever to complete the road repairs. However, Liu Bang really had a second army creeping through the passage of Chencang. This second army took Xiang Lu's fortress by surprise, and ushered in the Han Dynasty.

Watch the Fire Burn across the River

Sometimes, it is best to be the last one at the scene. When engaging in warfare, you may not be the only fighter. Sit back and let everyone else duke it out. Then you can swoop in when everyone else is exhausted and damaged from the fighting. You can pick up all of the pieces.

There are two benefits to waiting. The first is that you can appear like a friend. Your victim may just think that you are an ally, since you are not participating in the war. He will let you into his inner counsel and will trust you.

The second benefit is that everyone will be weakened by the time you make your attack. You will have almost no opposition when you move in. Some of the work will even be done for you.

This is particularly useful in occasions where an entire community engages in warfare on one person. It is also useful in situations where someone has elicited the hatred of several people. Let others ravage the victim's mind. Then come in with the coup de grace.

Hide a Knife behind a Smile

This is one the oldest tricks in the book. Smile and hide your metaphorical knife behind your back. Ingratiate yourself with your enemy by being sweet and seeming like an ally. Make your enemy trust you.

You will learn a lot about your enemy if you pretend to be his friend. You can use this information later to blackmail him. You can also find out what is dear to him, so that you can target it later. When he confides in you what he really wants in life, you will understand what to offer him to gain his full trust so that you can truly destroy him. But more than anything, being sweet lets you get into your enemy's most vulnerable presence. From there, you can do the most damage the most easily.

Betrayal deeply hurts. If you make your enemy view you as a friend, then you can hurt him even more than normal by betraying him. Loved ones and friends can inflict the deepest wounds.

Sacrifice the Plum Tree to Preserve the Peach Tree

Sometimes it is best to abandon any of your short-term goals to make way for a long-term goal. Some things are not as important as the ultimate end goal, so they can be forgotten and let go. For instance, if you are striving to destroy someone's reputation but you are losing credibility with your outrageous claims, abandon this sabotage to preserve your image. That way, you are more believable and you can actually continue to convince people of things about your victim later.

There is a rather brutal historic story behind this strategy. Cao Cao's army began to run out of food during the Three Kingdoms Period. He ordered the army captain to make the food stretch by diluting the rice with water. When the troops began to notice and complain, Cao Cao had the army captain killed and lied to everyone that the captain had been selling their rice to the enemy. The troops were fueled by fresh rage against the enemy and began to fight harder, even though their nutrition was suffering.

Take the Opportunity to Pilfer the Goat

Take advantage of any little possibility or opportunity. No opportunity is too small to offer you benefit. If your enemy demonstrates a weakness, take advantage of it promptly. Keep your plan flexible so that you can take advantage of opportunities.

Startle the Snake by Hitting the Grass around It

You do not ever want to reveal your intentions or your strategy. If you do so, you give your enemy the chance to prepare to fight you. Also avoid telling other people what your intentions are; you never know who is really your friend and who is out to sabotage you by being close to you. Keep your plans to yourself.

This way, you have the advantage of surprise. You can startle your enemy with an unannounced attack or betrayal.

Borrow Another's Corpse to Resurrect the Soul

Just like a corpse, some old technology, customs, or terms are now dead. You can borrow them to create a new form of attack that your enemy is not prepared for.

Letters are largely obsolete. You can use letter writing to harass your enemy or send him visual propaganda. What he thinks is a nice letter or post card from a friend is really just a form of propaganda. You can use friendly means to spread ideas and false news that will inspire terror in people, or else lead them to certain actions.

Entice the Tiger to Leave its Mountain Lair

Many people are protected by their positions. A good example is how a person is confident and protected from attack because of his ring of friends or his position of authority. To attack him, you must lure him away from his safety zone. Then he is vulnerable.

This method is the common tactic of murderers and child molesters. These people understand that taking someone aside is the best way to disable their defenses. You can use it to your advantage by taking someone away from his friends to weaken him mentally. He will be less likely to fight you off and he will be more vulnerable to your insinuations. For instance, if you tell someone that he is ugly around his friends, his friends will defend him and make him think that he is in fact handsome. But if you tell him this when you are alone and no one can stick up for him, he is more likely to believe you. The power of suggestion works better when you have someone alone.

In Order to Capture, One Must Let Loose

When you make someone feel trapped in a sticky deal or other form of imprisonment, then he is desperate to escape. He will put all of his energy into getting out of the deal and fleeing far, far away. He will not fight you as he attempts to escape. You can take the fight out of someone by offering the glimmer of hope that escape is possible. When the glimmer of hope turns out to be fake, your enemy will usually give up in despair. You have him totally trapped.

Use the false promise of escape as a way to break down morale and hope.

Tossing out the Brick to Get the Jade

Offer your enemy the promise of money, fame, sex, or power. These are huge temptations that almost everyone will fall for. By offering this promise to your enemy, you are giving him bait. If he takes it, he is falling into your trap. You now have control and your enemy owes you something in exchange for the bait you gave him.

Use the promise of something great to get your enemy to do something for you. For instance, if you want a bouncer to let you into a club, you can offer a monetary bribe. Bouncers are often underpaid and will accept some extra cash. You can manipulate people and gain power over them by promising them what they really want.

This proverb comes from a funny story. There was a poet named Chang Jian who wanted to learn from a greater poet, Zhao Gue. He heard that Zhao Gue would be at a local temple, so he went to the temple and wrote two lines of a four-line poem on the walls. When the master poet visited, the unfinished poem irked him and he completed the missing lines. From this, Chang Jian was able to learn more about poetry from a master. He tricked the master into teaching him by offering him the temptation of completing a poem and showing off talent to the masses.

Defeat the Enemy by Capturing the Chief

People always need a leader. A leader offers direction, morale, and support. When the leader is gone, the group will fall into chaos. They will no longer be able to fight and they will probably surrender. You can take advantage of the subsequent chaos for victory.

You can capture the leader in real life by sabotaging his reputation or making him resign from a leadership position. By disabling the chief, his followers will become powerless. Most likely, his group will dissolve.

Remove the Firewood under the Cooking Pot

By removing someone's source of strength, you can disable him. Just like if you remove the wood from a fire, he will have nothing to fuel his strength. Disable your enemy carefully by removing all of his support. Remove the people who love him. Remove his pride and his self-esteem. Remove his sense of reality. Using various manipulation strategies which are covered later, you can totally disable him. Isolation and smear campaigns can help remove his social support, while gaslighting and torture can remove his mental faculties and self-certainty.

Catch a Fish while the Water is Disturbed

Using confusion to weaken your enemy is an effective technique for disabling his defenses. You can use the most unexpected and inexplicable actions to disrupt your enemy's thinking and make him vulnerable. Use deliberate confusion to make people lose their faculties and their ability to defend themselves.

Slough off the Cicada's Shell

There will be times when you find yourself on the verge of defeat. When this happens, create the illusion that you are surrendering and giving up. Meanwhile, plan a secret attack. Your enemy will let his guard down, believing that he won, and that is when you can make your move.

It is always a great idea to let your enemy get full of himself. Let him think that he won. It may hurt your pride, but it enables him to lower his guard. Then you are sure to win.

Shut the Door to Catch the Thief

It is a great strategy to just completely destroy your enemy if you can. If you have information or something that will totally disable your enemy, use it. End the war once and for all. Do not ever hold back or let sympathy get the best of you.

It is not a bad idea to drop all pretense of kindness or friendship if you know for sure that you have the power to win the war. However, you only want to do this when you are confident that your plan of attack is sure to succeed. Do not hesitate and give your enemy time to collect his faculties. Just launch your attack immediately and be as brutal as you can.

Befriend the Distant State while Attacking the Neighbor

The people who work closely with you are more likely to be the people that you experience the greatest conflict with. Those who are further away from you often make better allies. Watch the people you are close to and never trust them. Meanwhile, find out who your allies really are.

They are probably people who are not as close to you. Use them to your advantage against your enemies. Collect a large gathering of allies that you can call on when you need them. Trust in the people who are satellites to you, rather than those that you really rely on.

This is especially helpful when you are using psychological warfare at work. The people you work closely with are the ones you rely on the most. Therefore, they can easily hurt you by letting you down. Never trust them and make sure that you have the support of other co-workers, should those you work closely with turn against you.

Obtain Safe Passage to Conquer the State of Guo

Borrow information or resources from an ally to attack your enemy. Then, use those same resources to attack the ally that you got them from. This keeps you ahead of everyone else. You will be the ultimate victor of everyone if you do not give anyone a break.

This refers to Chinese history, when a military leader used the state of Guo's offer of safe passage in order to turn against Guo and conquer it. This strategy is the epitome of betrayal and it is not very nice, but then psychological warfare is not supposed to be nice.

Replace the Beams with Rotten Timbers

This is self-explanatory. Replace the beams, or the main supports, of your enemy. Disrupt their way of doing things so completely that they fall apart. You can do this by disrupting someone's schedule, or by taking away the things that they rely on for support, such as a job. You can replace someone's timbers with rotten wood by getting them fired or otherwise disabling all of their supports in life. Never underestimate the way that people rely on routine and habit as a form of support. By taking away what gives their life meaning and structure, they become helpless and weak. You can then easily destroy them.

Point at the Mulberry Tree while Cursing the Locust Tree

Never clearly give names or obvious suggestions when you talk to other people, particularly your enemies. Hold even your closest allies at an arm's length. Use subterfuge when you impart information. This clears you from future blame, and it helps you be able to manipulate the truth in any way possible.

It is best to always keep everyone on a need-to-know basis. You do not need to share everything with everyone. By keeping things to yourself, you can easily gain control of a situation. Other people will be acting on false premises that they have gathered from the partial details you share. You can easily manipulate situations by providing limited details. Meanwhile, you can reserve control over others because you know something that they do not.

Play Dumb

Playing dumb is an age-old strategy. By making people think that you are dumb, you can make them underestimate you. They will set themselves up for attack and make themselves vulnerable because they trust that you are too stupid to make a move. They will not be prepared for when you suddenly emerge from the shadows with a brilliant attack.

Your genius is really another need-to-know detail that you should keep to yourself. Let everyone think that you are dumb. That way, you can rise up at unexpected moments and decimate your enemies when you need to. This can hurt your pride and this can be hard to fake dumbness, but it is very useful in the end.

Remove the Ladder when the Enemy has Ascended the Roof

You can lure someone into a situation where he has no friends or support. Then, remove his way back home to safety. In this way, you leave him weak and in a vulnerable place. In essence, you are cornering someone in a place where he has no defense.

You can do this physically or metaphorically. Physically, you can lure someone to a place where he has no allies. Then slash the tires on his car and leave him stranded. He will be defenseless and you will have the ultimate control over him. He may have to beg you for mercy to get home safely. You can use his vulnerability as a chance to force him to do something that you want in exchange for your help.

Metaphorically, you can make someone very uncomfortable by taking away all of his friends. Make life seem impossible for him. Soon, he will be begging for mercy and you can use the situation to your advantage.

Deck the Tree with False Blossoms

Just as fake blossoms can make a dying tree look healthy, you can make anything look the way you want it to. Using deceit and falseness, you can make your enemy feel threatened by something harmless, or believe that something useless is a valuable tool. You can shape someone's reality with falsehoods.

Part of psychological warfare calls for creating false realities for your enemies. You do this through propaganda, fake news, and other means. Convincing your enemy that something benign is to be feared can inject him full of fear over nothing.

For instance, if your enemy is a co-worker and your company gets a new boss, you can convince your co-worker that the new boss will be firing people and that his job is at special risk. He will become terrified of the new boss and the threat of losing his job for no reason at all. He may even quit.

You can also make someone humiliate himself. Convince him that a pretty girl is head over heels in love with him. Point out how she glances at him or how she postures herself. This will convince him to go after her. He will be shot down, and his ego will be hurt.

Make the Host and Guest Exchange Roles

Pretend to be someone's very best friend. This way, the person lets you in. You can use this opening in his heart to infiltrate him and defeat him. Playing nice and pretending to surrender is a classic way to stab someone in the back later.

You can use someone's friendship to glean information about someone. Friends talk. He will let his guard down and let you know very valuable details about himself, such as what he cares about and what he fears the most. You can then use this information to hurt him later. In addition, he will bring you around his loved ones. You can learn how to get to his loved ones in order to hurt him. You can get him to trust you with work projects and then fail him and blame the failure on him, so that he gets into trouble at work. Adjust your use of friendship to the situation and you will enjoy great success.

The Honey Trap

Use sexual seduction to get someone to make a mistake or to create discord within someone's life. You can try to seduce someone, or you can send a beautiful person to do the work for you. Either way, you can use sexual closeness to cause your enemy to make many blunders.

Most people are weak to sexuality, particularly when that sexuality boosts their ego. Therefore, the honey trap is sure to work. You can get your enemy to fall into many transgressions for sex. You can totally weaken him with the promise of sex with an attractive person.

The Empty Fort Strategy

If you think that your chances of defeat are low, then pretend that you are not interested in battle at all. Act nonchalant and innocent. Your enemy will lower his guard and think that you mean no harm. You will no longer be a perceived threat. Then, launch an attack on his mind when he is not prepared for it. The element of surprise can greatly increase your chances of victory.

Let the Enemy's Own Spy Sow Discord in the Enemy Camp

Through rumors and framing, you can make someone appear badly to their family, friends, lovers, and other loved ones. This will create discord between your enemy and his loved ones. It will disable his support network and make his life messy. Make sure to use very believable evidence when sabotaging someone's appearance to their loved ones.

Injure One's Self to Gain the Enemy's Trust

Pretend to hurt yourself. People will thus think that you are harmless, and that you can be trusted. They will feel sorry for you and will let their guards down as they attempt to help you. This is when you can spring like a cobra.

You can also pretend like your injury was caused by an enemy that both you and your enemy share. Then, the two of you can appear to be in collusion. Your enemy will think that you are an ally just to get back at the mutual enemy. In reality, you are not allies with anyone.

Combine Tactics

Never be afraid to combine tactics. The more tactics you use, the more likely your success will be. Combined tactics is a great way to confuse and batter someone mentally. Apply all of these tactics simultaneously to batter someone down, or one after another to weaken his defenses. Never be afraid to barrage several attacks; this can increase your chances of winning.

If All Else Fails, Retreat

You have to know when to surrender before you are destroyed. Some people are too formidable to break. If psychological warfare ends up causing you more harm than good, then consider retreating. It hurts to give up, but it can save your neck in the end.

Once you give up, that does not mean that the battle is forever finished. You can always launch a new attack later, when your enemy least expects it.

More Psychological Warfare Methods

Primary Targets

The primary targets in this psychological warfare are the reputation and the mind. You must focus more on these targets than anything else. By hitting these targets, you disable the enemy and win the war.

By harming someone's reputation, you accomplish a number of great things. For one thing, you are able to make this person seem to be of dubious credibility to the rest of the world. His or her sanity may be called into question. Thus, a person is at your mercy. You can do anything, and he or she cannot convince others that he or she is under attack. Also, by hurting one's reputation, you make one hurt. You tear away his or her prestige, job, and even trustworthiness. You make other people dislike the victim.

The mind is the next great target. By breaking your victim's mind, you cause him or her intense emotional discomfort and even pain. You cause him to doubt himself, or to hurt himself in an attempt to get rid of your influence. As a result, your victim will inadvertently ruin his life for you. You do not have to really do anything to hurt your victim. The beauty of psychological warfare is that he will do all of the work for you. You just have to hurt him mentally, rendering him unable to fight back and to think clearly.

Learn Your Enemy Well

Learn your enemy well. This should not be too hard, since usually your enemies are people that you once loved deeply. If you do not know your enemy well, you need to get to know them. Do this by any means necessary.

Knowing what scares your enemy is the single most important thing you must learn in order to successfully employ psychological warfare. Psychological warfare works best when it is used to stir up and rise the fears of your opponents.

Lower Intelligence

J.F.C. Fuller predicted that governments would partake in the gradual dumbing down of society by lessening educational efforts. As a result, people would become more malleable to propaganda because they would not know how to reason or think objectively. You can use this to your advantage and make the people around you feel dumb. Act like you have superior intelligence and they cannot possibly understand you. When people feel dumb, they are more likely to take your word for things.

Propaganda

Propaganda is a surprisingly effective tool for demoralizing and defeating enemies. The use of propaganda can spread ideas and emotions, such as fear. It can be used to stir up a mass hysteria. In more personal use, propaganda can be spread to individuals or entire communities to convince people of an idea that you want them to believe.

Propaganda takes many forms. Newspaper ads, flyers, and email messages are all great ways to spread propaganda. Social media makes it extremely easy to circulate propaganda ideas. For instance, as part of a social experiment, a myth about how people eat eight spiders a year while asleep was posted online. Quickly this myth circulated as credible information and now this misinformation is household knowledge. Many people believe that humans really do eat eight spiders a year in their sleep.

Create highly believable posts and write them with an authoritative voice. You may even claim that these posts or messages are from higher powers, like a made-up government agency. You will be surprised how people will accept this information as true if it has an authoritative tone to it. Most people accept what they are told and do not perform additional research or ask probing questions.

Propaganda is not always effective on everyone. Some people will ask questions and raise doubts. But if you can get your target individual or group to believe what you say, then you are doing well. You have influenced the thoughts of certain key people with your propaganda.

You want to train people to become information seekers so that they willingly expose themselves to propaganda of their own accord. Use positive reinforcement to reward people who ask you for information. This way, they will continue relying on you as a news source. You can thus shape the information they receive about the outside world and control their thoughts this way.

Learned Helplessness

Experiments on learned helplessness have revealed how strong this psychology is on people and animals. When a person learns that his or her best efforts are worthless and that fighting is futile, he or she will give up. He or she will then depend on others for help, handing over his or her independence. Even when the situation changes, someone is likely to still feel helpless because it is now a learned behavior and an approach to all of life that someone has learned.

A famous experiment with dogs called the Learned Helplessness Study illustrates this fact. In this study, scientists Mark Seligman and Steve Maier conducted this experiment on dogs in 1965. They put three different groups of dogs in harnesses. Group 1 was released from the harness after a few hours with no harm done to them. Group 2 was split into pairs, leashed together, and then given one shock administered by a small electric shock from a device that could be stopped by pressing on a lever. Dogs in the third group were also paired together and one dog was shocked, but pressing the lever on the device did not do anything to stop the shocks.

Later on, all the dogs from all three groups were placed in a box together. They were administered shocks at random while trapped in the box. The dogs could easily escape from these shocks simply by jumping through a door in the box. The dogs from Groups 1 and 2 hopped out of the box immediately to flee the pain of the shocks. The dogs from Group 3, however, had learned to be helpless and simply stayed in the box, seeming to believe that nothing could be done to escape the pain of the shocks. The Group 3 dogs only learned to jump out of the box when they were physically moved by the scientists at least two times. They had to be shown to escape their pain.

This study indicates that animals, and thus people, can learn to be helpless. If they think nothing can be done to avoid a bad situation, then they become complacent and do not help themselves, even when an obvious solution lies right under their noses. People who learn to be helpless become dependent on another person to help them learn how to overcome their issues.

If your victim cannot seem to do anything to escape from your unique brand of torture, then you can teach them helplessness. You can use learned helplessness to gain control over your victim. You can also use it to make your victim give up the struggle. Your victim will become dependent on you, putting you in a position of total control and power.

Discreditation

Discreditation is the process of tearing away someone's credibility. This can be accomplished through a variety of methods. The Internet and slander can be used to break down the victim's reputation in the eyes of others. Sleep deprivation and emotional manipulation can drive the victim to make a bad impression and appear crazy.

Discreditation works best with collusion between several people. These people can act like they do not care and are not personally involved in the warfare. They may be people in positions of authority, such as judges, cops, and mortgage lenders. Pretending to be disinterested third parties, they will thus leverage harsh judgments against someone. Their judgments can make a person question why they seem so repulsive and untrustworthy to other parties. This can crumble someone's credibility and reputation.

Discreditation tears down someone's reputation in public. But it also tears down the victim's sense of self. The victim begins to question his or her grasp on reality when all evidence seems to contradict what he or she sees. For instance, if he or she sees a conflict one way but a judge who is in collusion on the manipulation makes it clear that the conflict went down very differently, then the victim will wonder what reality really is. He or she will exist in a fragile place of doubt where he or she can easily be manipulated. Eventually, it will be easy to break the victim.

Self-destruction

It is easy to use psychological warfare to drive someone to self-destruction. Out of despair and desperation, someone may try to hurt him- or herself in response to psychological warfare. Usually they will end up in a psych ward or jail, and you will not be guilty of assault. Nevertheless, you were able to drive someone to self-harm.

By being unrelenting and merciless, you can give your victim the sense that he or she cannot get rid of you. If no one else believes his or her claims about psychological torture, then he or she will be alone and will feel like he or she is going crazy. Thus, he or she may attempt to kill him- or herself to get rid of you and the sensation of being crazy. He or she may even come to believe that cutting him or herself is a good way to get rid of you. If he or she is not successful in dying, then life is still practically over. Because of suicide laws, your victim will probably be locked away, and his or her credibility will further be eroded.

This can lead to poverty and homelessness when a person gets out of an institution. The person is now considered crazy and may even have a mental diagnosis. This makes employment and assimilating back into society hard. In addition, you can ramp up your psychological efforts to further break the person's sanity down further. The person will be insane by this point and truly unable to function as a normal member of society.

Thus, you have completely destroyed someone's life. You have driven them to self-harm and either death or poverty and homelessness. They have nothing that they used to have anymore.

Grid Awareness

Grid awareness is the network of people that are aware of psychological warfare. They may suspect or even know that psychological warfare is being conducted upon them. Their suspicions are often similar and they share views such as, "No one wants me to know about this. I could get in serious trouble if I run my mouth about it."

Grid awareness is an unfortunate clue that allows most people to realize that psychological warfare is very real and that is happening to them. It is evidence that psychological warfare really exists and really works. For anyone in doubt, a trip through underground websites and blogs dedicated to psychological warfare reveals how many people share eerily similar stories about their experiences. While these people do not know who is behind the warfare, they often surmise that it is their neighbors, family members, or even the CIA and NSA.

Unfortunately, grid awareness also poses a liability for people engaged in these tactics.

While you may never be caught outright, grid awareness can pose a problem. People can easily slip out from under your control if you are ever found out. They will become immediately defensive and they will attempt to block your attempts to control them. You must take steps to prevent this awareness from turning into mass hysteria or actual knowing. It is the only way to prevent grid awareness from exposing your covert operation.

First of all, be on the lookout for signs of awareness in your victims. Watch their social media posts and their blogs, if they have blogs. Also watch their behavior. Are they becoming excessively guarded, suspicious, unfriendly, or even outwardly defensive and hostile? Any rapid changes in behavior can suggest that they are beginning to suspect you.

You then need to stop engaging in warfare for a while. This is only a temporary setback in your operation. You can resume later. For now, you want to avoid confirming anyone's suspicions. Be polite and friendly and hold off on any unusual behavior. You want to avoid conspicuously dropping your typical mannerisms, however, so do not stop doing things you normally would. Just approach your victims without an ulterior motive for a while.

Try your best to make your victims feel like they are crazy. Make sure to use manipulation to suggest that they are crazy and that you are innocent of all accusations. Make them doubt their sanity by pointing out other things they are wrong about, or else indicating how innocent and good you are. Psychological warfare is already unbelievable and many people never suspect that it will happen to them. There is always an element of doubt when it comes to grid awareness. Exploit that doubt. Also exploit the fact that there is no solid proof against you.

Discredit their reputations, if need be. You do not want others to believe what they are saying. Of course, most people already find claims to psychological mind control hard to believe, so you have that advantage in defending yourself. Most people already will be inclined to disbelieve and discredit your victims' claims. They will assume that your victims are developing paranoid schizophrenia. Nevertheless, there will always be a few people that might resonate with their claims and believe what they are saying. You can add extra security by leaking information in a secondhand manner, such as through the Internet, that will discredit and tear down your victims' reputations. You can also set them up to look like fools in public, thus tearing down their public reputations. Ideally, you will do this even before you begin the psychological warfare attack.

With these steps, you can probably protect yourself from discovery. It is very important that you never get caught. Fortunately, the likelihood of you getting caught is very low. Psychological warfare is typically not detectable to most people. It is also not likely to leave clues or evidence. Only you can understand your motives and what you are doing, so others are perfectly likely to never find out what you are up to. Even suspicion can be dismissed and decimated.

Planting Ideas

Using exposure to ideas can make your enemy come to accept these ideas. Then, when the ideas become reality, your enemy is less likely to fight them.

Hitler and other political leaders are notorious for using media, such as plays, to accustom the population to certain horrible ideas. Hitler would use disturbing plays to plant ideas into the minds of the German population. After watching a disturbing play, for instance, people would become desensitized. No harm came to them from the ideas contained in the play, so they decided that there was no harm to these ideas. When Hitler then began introducing these ideas to the military, no one raised concerns.

You can employ this to your own psychological warfare. Expose people to horrible ideas through hypothetical conversation, Youtube videos, TV shows, or other media. People will come to accept the ideas as fairly harmless. They will not fight you as much once you make the ideas reality.

Chapter 3: Psychological Torture

Psychological torture is useful to know about. Torture is always a side effect, or even a rudimentary part, of warfare. Since the very beginning of human warfare, people have used torture on enemies to break them down. Torture is a useful way to glean information and it is a useful way to break someone down mentally.

While you may never have someone bound and gagged in your secret underground dungeon for torture purposes, understanding ways to make the mind break can give you useful ideas for psychological warfare. You can find ways to employ methods like sensory overload to make your enemy go crazy.

Also, if you ever do have someone bound and gagged in your underground dungeon, you will know what to do. While physical torture is not a good idea, there may be situations in life where you can actually use it. Take care because torture is not legal. It is also rarely truly necessary for your home use of psychological warfare.

Psychological torture sometimes uses physical means to hurt an enemy's mind. However, psychological torture methods focus entirely on breaking the human mind and hurting someone mentally. Using fear, humiliation, and sensory manipulation, you can make someone break. You can cause him to question his ability to perceive reality and disable his confidence in himself. You can also make someone do whatever you want to escape the horrible emotions that you are inflicting upon him.

Many of the following torture methods are employed by the CIA and Department of Defense on political prisoners. They are tried and true methods to break people into making confessions. They are also quite useful for disabling your enemy's mental fortitude and sanity. By driving someone crazy, you can hurt them, discredit them, and disable them as a viable threat to your war effort. After I finish covering these methods, I will provide you with a section on realistic adaptations of torture for normal home use. You can adapt the following methods to your own use in any way that you see fit. One thing about torture is that it can be fun for you to employ.

Common Torture Methods

Sensory Deprivation

Sensory deprivation calls for one or more of a subject's senses to be completely cut off. Any and all stimulation of that particular sense is removed. You may remove someone's sight, hearing, or even sense of touch. Depriving stimulation to all of the senses works even more efficiently. You can cut off all of someone's sensory faculties to totally disable his sanity and his perception of the world.

The human brain requires sensory stimulation to maintain its view of the world and its understanding of reality. Being deprived of these glimpses of reality through the sensory organs can make the brain lose its perception and proper understanding. The brain easily turns to confusion and hallucinations as it attempts to manufacture sensory stimulation and some sort of reality to replace what is missing. Sometimes, this loss of reality is permanent. You can permanently break someone mentally with sensory deprivation. They will never be the same, as many survivors of this torture can attest.

Monotony in sensory stimulation can also have the same effect as sensory deprivation. A monotone sound or other stimulation that remains constant and static creates what is known as the "ganzfeld effect." This effect is identical to the effect of sensory deprivation. People cannot handle hearing or seeing the same exact stimulus for too long. It can lead to total focus on the stimulus, which is the same as sensory deprivation.

To illustrate how serious sensory deprivation is, let's virtually visit a room that is known as the quietest room in the world. This room is located at the Orfield Laboratories in Minneapolis, Minnesota. It is ninety-nine point nine percent sound absorbent, making it the quietest manmade structure in the world. Nobody has been able to stay in this room past forty-five minutes. Just standing in the room for a long period of time induces crazy hallucinations. If you force a prisoner to stay in such a room for past forty-five minutes, you can break his mind forever.

Sensory Overload

Sensory overload is the exact opposite of sensory deprivation, and it works just as well. Exposing someone to too much stimulation of any one of their senses can result in sensory overload. You can blast someone with too much noise, strobe lights, or other stimulus to drive them crazy. Overloading all of their senses is especially effective.

Sensory overload makes people become irritable, lethargic, and overwhelmed very quickly. They will be unable to concentrate and will be irritated easily, even by tactile stimulation, such as their own clothing. They may go nuts and become seriously violent, even to themselves. Lengthy exposure can lead to hallucinations and post-traumatic stress disorder, a permanent reaction to a traumatic event.

It is believed that residents of cities suffer from a minor form of sensory overload. This causes city dwellers to be more anxious and irritable than people from calmer environments.

Sleep Deprivation

The effects of sleep deprivation became public during a publicity stunt in 1959, when a Top 40 radio personality named Peter Tripp challenged himself to go two hundred hours without sleep. The stunt was meant to benefit the March of Dimes, but it ultimately revealed the effects of sleep deprivation on the human brain.

After just a few days of staying awake, Tripp began to hallucinate, and by forty hours, he required chemical help to remain awake and functional. While Tripp did not sustain permanent damage from this "Wake-a-Thon," he made it clear how harmful lack of sleep can be. Others who have attempted (sometimes successfully) to beat his record, such as the high school student Randy Gardner who made it two hundred and sixty-four hours awake, have all experienced hallucinations as well. The psychosis associated with stimulant abuse is partly attributed to sleep deprivation.

Because of its devastating effects on the human mind, sleep deprivation is a useful psychological torture technique. Keeping someone awake by thwarting their attempts to sleep or administering stimulants such as amphetamines can successfully mentally break the person. After so many hours, they will begin hallucinating and will not be able to maintain their grasp of reality.

Mock Executions

Staging the execution of a person can lead to extreme terror that successfully breaks a person. A person may be led to believe that he is being led to his own execution, or he may be forced to watch the fake execution of someone he loves or a fellow prisoner from his cause. Seeing someone die or believing that he is about to die will cause him to break down in terror. He may even utter a desired confession.

People are programmed to balk at the sight of harm to another human being. You can create hysteria in a person by exposing him to the deaths of others, even if the deaths are fake. You can thus get someone to lose control of himself out of terror.

White Torture

White torture combines sensory deprivation and isolation, creating the perfect torture method. Subjects are typically unable to withstand white torture very long before they forget their own identities or how to interact socially. The damage is typically permanent.

White torture is typically conducted in an environment that is entirely white. There are white walls, white furniture, and even white rice served on white plates. Prisoners only see the color white. Britain has been known to use white noise as well. This monotony in sensory stimulation causes the ganzeld effect that I discussed before.

There is a survivor of white torture who describes the long-term effects that white torture has had on his mental health. He cannot sleep without taking sedatives and he still feels very lonely, even years later. He is so lonely because he cannot feel comfortable with himself or initiate social interaction and relationships with other people.

The pain and craziness that white torture causes often leads to prisoners and victims confessing. Even if they are not guilty, people will confess to crimes just to avoid the mind-numbing loneliness and horror of white torture.

Chinese Water Torture

Chinese water torture, also known as Spanish water torture, is a method of torture that drips water onto someone's bare skin to induce terror and psychosis. Humans are given to believe from experience that water creates hollows in the ground, so they think that the continually dripping water will form a hollow on their forehead. The sensory stimulation of the dripping water is also incredibly repetitive, leading to sensory overload. These two emotions combined can lead to great suffering in victims.

Waterboarding

Waterboarding is a drowning simulation. The subject is strapped to a board, with his head facing up, and then he is dunked into water or else water is poured down his air passages. The temporary experience of drowning is so unpleasant that it will sometimes cause people to break down and confess during interrogations. Fear of death and the desire to escape the unpleasant circumstances can lead to victims breaking down to escape.

Hooding

Hooding involves covering someone's head with a dark, heavy hood. The victim does not know what is happening to him and his breath and sight are restricted. He will feel mounting dread and terror. It can be useful to attack or pretend to attack other prisoners around him, leading him to think that he is about to be beaten. Hooding has also long been used on prisoners that are about to be hung or executed. It leads to mounting dread of the upcoming execution, compounding the terror of death that they already feel.

Half-Hanging

Half-hanging involves tightening a rope around a victim's neck until the victim passes out from oxygen deprivation. The victim is then revived and the process is repeated. The terror of oxygen deprivation is instinctual and inherent to everyone. Also, the repeated lack of oxygen can have damaging effects on the human brain. Therefore, someone who does not have oxygen will be more likely to confess. Victims will want to end the half-hanging as soon as possible, which drives them to confess as well.

Walling

Walling is where subjects are fitted with a collar. They are then repeatedly slammed into a wall by the collar. They bounce off of the wall by their shoulders and sustain only bruising. Typically only a rubber wall is used. This is because physical harm is not the desired effect of this torture. However, the sensation of being flung around can be terrifying and dizzying. This can make prisoners eventually crack. It gives the torturer the ultimate control.

Electric Shock Torture

While electric shock torture is physical, it can create fear and humiliation in victims. As the pain of shocks increase, victims often lose control of their bowels and bladders. This causes them great humiliation while also pain. They are likely to break down and confess after some electric shock is use.

Parrilla is a form of electric shock torture that involves hooking people up to a metal grill and essentially frying them with electricity. Often electrodes are attached to the victim's nipples and genitalia and temples, the most sensitive places in the human body. This makes *parrilla* both painful and humiliating.

Nuremburg Plate

Most commonly used in the medieval ages, the Nuremburg Plate is a massive Merry-go-round-like torture device that is in the shape of a wheel. Subjects are chained to the plate by their arms and legs and then spun in a circle. The spinning leads to disorientation, dizziness, and vomiting in victims. It is extremely unpleasant and also makes victims feel powerless.

The Nuremburg Plate was only used inside the Nuremburg Castle in Bavaria, Germany. Supposedly, it was never used outside of Nuremburg Castle. It was typically used on regal perpetrators who were suspected of treason.

Starvation

Starvation can involve either denying someone food altogether or telling a prisoner that his food is poisoned so that he will refuse to eat it or will throw it up. While the human body can survive for many weeks without food, starvation can make people crazy and desperate. They will often confess or surrender just to eat. They are not able to maintain their mental faculties for very long while severely undernourished.

Starvation is how people have been able to besiege enemies or end strikes. It is also often used on POWs. Starving someone out turns into a race between the person's will and your patience. If your patience is endless, then you really can starve someone until he breaks.

Tarring and Feathering

Tarring and feathering used humiliation to destroy prisoners. People would be captured, smothered in tar, and then rolled in feathers. The feathers and tar would be uncomfortable, but the real torture lay in the humiliation that the victims would then experience as they were forced to parade around in public. People would often jeer at them and throw things at them. The public jeering created a terrible psychological torture for the victims of tarring and feathering.

Bamboo Torture

Bamboo torture was chiefly used in Asia during WWII, when prisoners of war were tied up and suspended above thickets of bamboo. Since bamboo is very fast-growing, it was only a matter of time before the young shoots grew tall enough to pierce the suspended prisoners' bodies. Bamboo shoots are very sharp and inflicted great pain and even death upon prisoners. The psychological aspect of this torture lay in the fact that prisoners had to suspend in the air for days, anticipating slow, unavoidable pain. Sometimes they would surrender before the bamboo could actually pierce them.

Abacination

Abacination involves slowly blinding someone over time. Using a chemical drip that eats away eye tissue, prisoners must stand there and tolerate the gradual loss of their vision. As the world grows dark around them, they often break down and confess out of terror. You can drive someone crazy permanently this way by traumatizing the person.

Adapting Torture for Home Use

Many of the above torture methods are not practical for personal use. It is impossible to conduct these methods of torture undetected. You could get in trouble for assault if you are caught using these methods. However, you can take these torture methods and adapt them for more practical home use.

Using the concepts above, you now understand that messing with a person's senses is an ideal way to harm them and make them question reality. It is easy to employ sensory deprivation or overload in real life without trying very hard. Threatening people with terror or impending death also works well to gain control over them. Keep these facts in mind as you design your own personal torture methods.

Repetition

As you saw in the previous section about torture, repetition of a stimulus can drive someone insane. The slow drip drop of water, for instance, can make someone start to go crazy, become irritable, and even start hallucinating. It can drive someone to self-harm or even suicide.

It is not always possible to trap someone in a torture chamber and expose them to a constant stimulus. But you can still get to them by putting a constant stimulus in their home or car. Think of the things that drive people crazy naturally. Many people are intolerant of the sound of people chewing food. Dogs licking themselves is another sound that people cannot tolerate. Dripping water certainly has an adverse effect on people. White torture is so effective because of the repetition of the color white and white noise. You can use this understanding to develop a foolproof torture device that makes someone go crazy.

Watch how quickly people become vicious when their neighbors drive them crazy with repetitive noise, such as hammering nails into a roof or playing loud music that utters a distinctive bass thump. Neighborly relations will quickly become strained. You can use this natural aversion to noise to your advantage and create a constantly annoying presence if you are performing warfare on your neighbors.

One problem with this, however, is that you will not just target the neighbor you wish to torture, but you also will affect others. Your torture will be witnessed by other people, which is never a good thing in psychological warfare.

Another problem is that you may be subject to legal noise complaints. It is a great idea to emit a constant, annoying noise and then shut it off before the police or a landlord is called to investigate. People will tell your neighbors that the noise does not appear to exist. Your neighbors will begin to wonder if they are crazy.

You can also drive someone crazy by installing a device that emits some sort of high-pitched frequency inside their home. Installing the same sound in their car can further aggravate them and make the torture successful. There are devices available online that utter high-pitch frequencies to repel bats. You can also purchase white noise machines. White noise machines are often used in white torture, which is quite effective.

A low, steady hum can be very effective. Many people report hearing hums in certain parts of the world, including Taos, New Mexico, and Bristol, England. These hums are unexplained sounds that arise from the Earth itself. There is no scientific explanation for them. Creating such a mystery hum for your victim can be safely blamed on Earth hums.

There are countless reports of mystery noises driving people crazy. The mysterious hum is one of the noises that both puzzles and enrages people who must listen to it constantly.

You do not just have to use sound, either. You can use visual cues. Exposing someone to the same visual stimulus constantly can truly irritate and even hurt them. Flashing lights or repeated propaganda images are two forms of visual stimulus that can be repetitive. You can use something like a disco ball to create flashing light that can drive someone crazy.

Saying the same thing to someone over and over can mentally break them. People will quickly become enraged if you keep saying the same thing over and over. The lack of differentiation in stimulus and the perceived insult that people feel repeating yourself has on their intelligence can make repeating yourself drive someone crazy.

Isolation

It may not be practical to isolate someone you know in a torture chamber or sensory deprivation tank. But you can isolate someone emotionally and socially, particularly if that someone is close to you. If someone is close to you, you can slowly demand that he stop seeing his friends and family. You can fabricate stories and point out past hurts that will make the person not want to see friends and family anymore. Tell him that he is better than the people he loves and that he does not deserve how they treat him. Show him little examples where his friends and family have hurt him or failed to appreciate him.

You can also create geographical distance to widen the emotional void that you are working to create. Use a strategic move to another area as an excuse to draw someone away from his loved ones. Over time, he will slowly stop talking to family and friends.

You also need to prevent him from developing new friends. You can do this by limiting his access to the outside world. Live somewhere remote and leave someone with no car or way to get out. Limit and always supervise outside interaction. When someone leaves the house, always be there and dominate conversation so that he cannot talk to other people. Over time, you can begin to make someone afraid of the outside world by telling him stories of how awful people are and how scary the world is. When your victim happens to wander outside, set up tragic or terrible events that will scare him and make him associate the outside world with pain. Your victim will develop agoraphobia and want to stay inside all the time, out of terror.

By isolating someone completely, you can make him lose the social contacts that helps cement his sanity and his self-image. He will begin to lose a part of himself in isolation. With no one to tell him who he is, he will begin to come unglued while in isolation. His composure will melt away as he becomes crazy and desperate. He will start to hallucinate and believe anything that you tell him. He will rely on you entirely for everything.

People also become entirely dependent on their captors for social contact, and you can use this to your advantage. With no one to point out your abuse, you can make your victim rely on you completely. Your victim will no longer have a social point of reference for how people should act, so he will begin to accept your abuse and torture as normal. He will rely on you for news and ideas and affirmation that what he is doing is correct. Tell him whatever you want him to hear so that he becomes your perfect puppet.

Threats

Threats are one of the oldest and most effective ways to get what you want out of someone. By threatening someone's safety or loved ones, you can gain control over his emotions and get him to do what you want. You can also damage his sense of security and remove his feeling of safety. You can instill fear that lowers his quality of life quite thoroughly.

The best threat for home use is not against someone's physical well-being. You can be arrested for physical threats. Rather, your threat should be against someone's sanctity and reputation. Blackmail is your friend in this situation. If you can glean some pertinent information about someone that will damage his reputation, use it as a threat to control him and get him to do what you demand. If you cannot find dirt on someone, make up some credible information and manufacture proof to create a successful smear campaign. Making up information can work, but almost everyone has some sort of dirt in their pasts. You can easily gain control of someone with the smallest embarrassing details that can shatter his reputation and even drive away his family.

It is a good idea to get very intimate with the people whom you want to blackmail. This increases your chances of them confiding in you or doing something shameful around you. Get to know their family and friends. Position yourself conveniently wherever they are so that you can innocently spy on them. Do research into their past, perhaps posing as a private investigator or other person to retrieve stories about them from old employers, professors, and even classmates and old friends. If they have enemies, quietly and discreetly meet with their enemies to get further dirt on them. You will be surprised at how willing people are to talk about others. Gossip can help you glean a lot of information.

In dire situations, you can also employ threats of financial instability or harm to a person's loved ones and pets. However, these blatant threats are rarely as effective because you are less likely going to be able to act on them. Blackmail is a far easier way to threaten someone successfully.

Harassment

In 1974, Bashir Kouchacji was captured and tortured in Beirut because of a political misunderstanding. He later left his native Lebanon to open the Marrakesh Restaurant in Washington, D.C. Just when he believed that life was good again, he began to receive constant bizarre, threatening phone calls at his restaurant in 1983. The caller would threaten him and extort him for money, while using countless different voices. The calls followed him wherever he went: his home, his work, Marrakesh's sister restaurant, even hotels where he traveled. When the FBI traced the calls, they found that the calls were coming from numerous different pay phones all over the city. The calls came at such a frequency, often from different locations at the same time, that many people had to be involved in the plot.

As a result of this harassment, Kouchacji began to suffer nightmares. Eventually, he went crazy and was admitted to a psychiatric hospital. Since then, he has never been quite right. The calls still come at times and Kouchacji sometimes has to return to the hospital to get some peace. The calls literally drove him insane.

This story illustrates how frequent and relentless harassment can destroy someone's sanity and happiness. One can easily employ intense harassment as a weapon of psychological torture and warfare. You can use threatening phone calls, notes, emails, and letters to drive someone crazy. You can also make sure that the source of the harassing correspondence is untraceable so that you are never caught and charged with harassment.

Stalking

Stalking is a form of harassment that involves the use of fear and the threat of bodily harm. You can employ stalking as a means to traumatize someone. When you stalk people, you fill their lives with fear and make them afraid to even turn out their lights at night. You create a permanent presence that robs people of their peace and their ability to focus on living their lives. Stalking can greatly lower a person's quality of life and cause them great psychological harm, and as a result it is a great and powerful form of psychological torture.

If you are untraceable as a stalker, you can also make someone feel as if they are going crazy. No one else will believe them when they claim that they are being stalked. Even the police will not help them. Yet you can continue gaining complete control over them. It is estimated that most victims will put up with one hundred incidences of stalking before even going to the police. Therefore, you may be able to do much damage before the risk of legal action even arises.

In one case, a young special-needs teacher ended a brief romance with an over controlling pharmacist. The pharmacist began to flood her phone with obscene texts and calls. He would appear at her school and follow her home, even knocking on her door at three a.m. He always seemed to be watching her. The young woman quickly developed severe anxiety issues and had thoughts of suicide. Her problems have lasted many months later. This is an example of how profoundly stalking can hurt people.

One way you can use stalking to your advantage is by making your actions look like that of some paranormal being. You can cause someone intense misery while discrediting their reputations.

Gaslighting

Gaslighting will be covered in greater detail in the following chapter. This is a great method for making someone question his own intelligence and feel like he is breaking or going insane. You can use gaslighting as a form of torture without even seeming like you are torturing someone. It is easy to employ gaslighting on people that you see often.

To understand what gaslighting is, first I will explain where the term came from. In the 1930s, a rather disturbing play came out where an emotionally abusive husband would turn the gaslights in his house down low. When his wife claimed that the house seemed darker, he informed her that the gaslights were at a normal level and that she was imagining things. Later, he began to tell her that men who came by to investigate the family were figments of her imagination. She began to question her own sanity and fell apart. She felt crazy and found that life was extremely unpleasant.

You can thus make people question their sanity by telling them the opposite of what they think is true. In an extreme example, try telling them that it is sunny when it is obviously rainy. Usually, however, gaslighting is far more subtle. Gaslighters will claim that someone is making up everything that was said in the course of a conversation, for instance. Constantly contradicting someone on all of their senses can make them start to question if their perception is true. It is a good way to undermine someone's self-assurance.

Gaslighting works best on loved ones and people that you are around often. Isolation helps in these cases because you can protect your victim from other sources that confirm that he or she is not actually going crazy. Social support can help people recover from gaslighting, so limit social contact.

Stirring up Fear

You can make someone feel intensely unsafe by playing with his natural propensity for fear. By stirring up fear in someone, you can make his life unpleasant. But you can also seem like you are simply a caring Good Samaritan, just watching out for him. Use the power of suggestion to plant ideas in someone's mind about the unsafety of the world. Tell stories about how unsafe the neighborhood or how unsafe his house is. Tell him that people were murdered in his house. These things will make him feel threatened and uneasy, and it will torture him with fear. You can ruin his comfort in his own home and drive him crazy with fear.

Chapter 4: Manipulation

Manipulation is the art of subtly influencing people to do what you want. It grants you control over people mentally and emotionally. Using a variety of subtle techniques, you can gain vast power over the minds of others. You can then use this power to your advantage.

Manipulation is undoubtedly one of the best tools for getting your way. People are not always willing to do your bidding. You do not have to accept no for an answer, however. You can simply use manipulation to ensure your success. Get people to inadvertently do what you want.

You can also use manipulation as a means to hurt and mentally break people. By weaving a tight web of negative emotions around someone, emotions such as fear and inadequacy, you can cripple someone's will. People will become reliant on you for their emotional well-being. They will also begin to doubt their sanity.

Manipulation is one of the main cornerstones of psychological warfare. You cannot perform psychological warfare if you do not know how to gain control over someone's mind. This chapter is your guide to gaining this subtle yet powerful control.

FOG

When using manipulation, use a combination of fear, obligation, and guilt to create an emotional web that will trap a person. Inject fear into him. Then act sweet, so that he feels obligated to help you. If he ever goes against your wishes, use guilt to make him feel terrible. You can even hurt yourself to get him to stay and serve you longer.

These three emotions are essential when you are using psychological warfare. You want to keep someone in a constant state of one of these three emotions in order to exert control. Known as FOG, these emotions literally create a fog over someone's judgment.

Conceal Your Intent as Goodwill

To successfully manipulate a person, you must take care to disguise your true intentions. Nobody will want to do anything for you if they know that you are up to no good. Therefore, you must conceal your intent as goodwill. Make people believe that you mean the best. Show people that you care and that you are simply looking out for them. Do good and kind things to make it seem like you are just a Good Samaritan. In reality, you are just doing things to ingratiate yourself with your victims. But no one has to know this.

Making Someone an Offer that they can't Refuse

When you want to gain control over someone, you must make him want to give you control. The best way to do this is to offer something that he really wants. This could be money, security, or love. This could be flattery and ego boosting. Most people do want to be loved, so you can often use affection and the promise of unconditional love as a means to gain control over people. Sex is also often a powerful motivator for human behavior and offering good sex is a tantalizing offer that many people will not be able to refuse. The reasons that sex and love work so well is because they boost a person's self-esteem. A person relies on self-esteem to feel good. If you always make someone feel good, then he will want to come back to you for more. He will do anything to please you so that he can keep getting this sensation of being loved and wanted from you.

It is important to read a person to learn what he really desires. If he mentions that he wants someone to help him stop feeling so lonely, be that person who makes him not feel lonely. If he mentions that he just wants money, offer him money-making opportunities that will help him exponentially.

Power of Suggestion

The power of suggestion is just that, a power. The things you say to someone can really have a great bearing on their psyche. By making certain suggestions, you can manipulate someone into thinking exactly what you want him to think.

The power of suggestion works on changing someone's self-concept. Through a few small, meaningful hints, you can make someone doubt his self-concept. He will start to wonder if there is truth to what you have said. He may begin to believe you, especially if life continues to reinforce the words that you have uttered.

You can tell someone that he will never be a good father. He will thus develop doubt and insecurity about his fatherhood. Each of his normal failures in parenthood will act to reinforce this belief, until he has absolutely no faith in his capability as a dad. His beliefs will become a self-fulfilling prophecy.

Exploit Fear

The flip side to promising someone what they want is to threaten them with what they fear the most. You can exploit someone's fears and insecurities to gain control over him. Listen to what someone says to find out what scares him the most, and you have some very pertinent information about someone. You have a weakness that you can now exploit.

There are two ways that you can use someone's own fear against him. The first way is to threaten someone with what he fears the most to keep him from leaving the safety of your affection. If someone fears ageing, for instance, you can claim that he will grow old alone if he ever leaves you. You can point out his wrinkles or his few gray hairs all the time, so that he feels old and believes that no one will want to be with him now. As a result, he will stay with you and tolerate your manipulation.

Another use for someone's fear is when you want to influence someone. If you do not want someone to do something, for instance, use his fear of failure to convince him that he will fail so he will not try anything. Threaten someone with his own fears to make him submit to your will.

You can make someone feel unsafe in his own home as a form of psychological warfare. Use the power of fear to manipulate someone by telling him horror stories about the neighborhood or about electric fires and other catastrophes. You can make him so fearful that he will be more likely to do your bidding. He may even move away.

Emotional Blackmail

Emotional blackmail uses the fear, obligation, and guilt that are required to successfully manipulate someone. You basically use fear, obligation, and guilt to make someone feel like they owe you and they must do what you want. Should someone fail to do what you want, you can threaten to hurt him or the ones he loves, badly.

You can use all sorts of threats. Read a person well to determine what threats will work. Usually, threats of withdrawing love work the best. Threats against someone's family are also usually highly successful. You can use what he cares about as a bargaining tool or a threatening device.

Psychological warfare can also use literal blackmail. If some sort of truth would hurt someone should it leak, then you can use that truth as a means to get your way. "I will tell everyone about..." is a good threat to hold over someone's head. Make sure to gain as much information about people as you can. The threat of blackmail will make them scramble to do your bidding.

Passive-Aggressive Behavior

Passive-aggressive behavior allows you to act aggressively, without getting caught. You act in a way that makes others find it impossible to confront you for any specific behavior. Nevertheless, you are still able to express aggression and create a lingering fear of your anger. Passive-aggressive behavior is sneaky and non-direct.

You can use all sorts of indirect methods to express your anger and hostility. You can sulk and act sullen, you can refuse to do tasks, and you can conveniently "forget" about important things, such as birthdays. You can also leave passive aggressive notes or messages that say things like, "I worked really hard on this so it would be nice if everyone respected what I did." Making snide comments designed to hurt someone, without actually insulting them, is another way to be passive-aggressive. You might dismiss someone's hard work or someone's feelings. You can pretend to compliment someone, when really you are insulting them. Basically, you want to always mask your anger.

Gossiping

Gossiping is one of the most essential weapons of psychological warfare. Just as the military has certain kinds of guns, you must have certain weapons. Gossiping is one that you are required to have. Gossiping enables you to accomplish two things: discredit someone and make someone intensely uncomfortable.

By spreading stories about someone, you can get everyone to hate him. You can create a negative, uncomfortable environment of hostility. No one likes to know that others are talking about them without their knowledge. It creates a sense of paranoia and unhappiness. Use this to your advantage to make an environment practically unbearable to someone with clandestine gossip.

You can also make it clear to someone that you are not happy with him without telling him yourself. Other people will tell him for you. He will change his actions after hearing about the horrible things that you have been saying about him behind his back. You never have to say a word. This is a form of passive aggressive behavior.

Changing the Energy of a Room

You can change the energy of a room by being sulky, embarrassing, or dramatic. You're horrible, childish behavior will make the person that you are trying to manipulate feel so uncomfortable that he will do anything just to get you to stop. You can also make the situation that he is in so unbearable that he will leave.

Many kids employ this on their parents by screaming and crying when they are bored. They know that their parents will get uncomfortable and leave to comfort them. You can behave childishly too and it will probably work. For instance, if someone wants to go to a party, you can come along, but act like a baby and pout the whole time. You will drag the mood of the party down so low that your companion will probably leave just to get you to stop being so ugly.

But be aware that this can damage your own reputation. Other people will think less of you if you act like a child.

Keep The Focus on the Other Person

No one likes to just sit there listening to you talk about yourself. People prefer to go on and on about themselves. Therefore, you can get someone to like you by letting them talk about themselves ceaselessly. Ask them questions to show your fake interest, and pretend to hang on their every word. People will think that you are wonderful. You want to maintain this wonderful, selfless image when running manipulation on anyone. You will seem like the most dazzling person in the room.

In addition, you can glean a lot of information about people when you let them talk. You can find out fears and likes they have that you can later exploit if you need. Pay careful attention to people when they talk to you. You never know what could be a useful weapon later on.

Make Others Feel like they are in Control

When you are performing psychological warfare, you want to be in total control. But few people like to knowingly relinquish control. Therefore, you can be very stealthy and ingratiating by letting someone feel like he is in control. This will disguise how much you are really in control.

Let your victim think that he is in control by letting him know that he is. Answer to his every bidding, while guilting him. Strive to please him. Make him feel like you value his thoughts and opinions. Flatter him and tell him that the world is at his feet.

Reverse Psychology

Make it appear to your victim that you do not want him to do something, when in fact you do. He will then feel like he is in control and he is defying you when he does what he thinks you don't want. Your enemy will never know that he fell into your trap, and you will get him to do what you want without seeming like you are in control at all.

A good example is when you tell your husband, "Don't you dare get pizza. You'll get fat." Meanwhile, you secretly want him to get fat so that no one else will want to date him. He will sneak pizza to defy you and will put on the weight that makes him so unattractive to other women.

Sharing Ideas

Make it look like you had the same idea for something as someone else. This affirmation makes your enemy feel like he is supported. He will then take the action that you both apparently thought of simultaneously.

For instance, if you want a co-worker to mention that it may be more efficient to do a project at work a certain way and you recognize that you will somehow benefit from him doing it that way, mention, "Oh, yes, I thought that too." Then he will feel more confident doing the project that certain way because you agreed with him.

Increments

Incrementally warm people up to your ideas. Expose someone to your ideas slowly over time, and he will gradually come to accept them as normal. He will put up less resistance if you warm him up to the idea over time, rather than if you force ideas on him immediately. When you force ideas on people, they are more likely to become shocked and say no. This is why gradual exposure is so useful.

If someone says no, don't give up. Just start to gradually drop hints. Expose him to the idea. Eventually, he will probably come around to the idea.

Conditioning

Conditioning is typically associated with Pavlov's famous experiments with dogs. Pavlov conditioned the dogs in his experiment to salivate at the sound of the bell. They associated the bell with receiving food. You can condition people in a likewise manner. By teaching them to have associations between a stimulus and a reward, they will perform a certain action.

One way you can do this is playing someone's favorite music whenever he performs a chore for you. He will come to associate the sound of his music to doing the chore. Soon, you won't even have to ask. You just put on his favorite song, and he will snap to cleaning.

Conditioning is a great way to get people you know well to do things for you. You can subtly train them to do your bidding without even having to say a word. It may take some time to train someone, but usually conditioning works fairly quickly. Just be consistent in your stimulus and your reward and you will start to see results.

Positive Reinforcement

Positive reinforcement is where you reward behavior that you desire so that you can encourage it. You want to give someone some sort of positive, enjoyable stimulus so that he will want to keep performing a desired behavior for you. You can just tell someone thank you, or you can offer them something they enjoy, such as their favorite ice cream. Use the promise of what someone really wants to motivate them to do what you want. People will come to associate pleasing you with getting a pleasurable reward, so they will become trained, like dogs.

Keep the Spotlight Trained on You

In psychological warfare, you want to maintain dominance in every situation. Therefore, you want to always remain at the center of attention. Dismiss other people's pain and rights to attention so that you can keep the spotlight trained on you at all times. Always steal the show from everyone else to remain at the center of attention.

For instance, if someone has a bad headache, claim that you have a much worse one but you are tolerating it without crying and whining. Do what you can to appear both dominant and more of a victim than the other person. Never let another person get the upper hand by getting more attention than you.

By keeping a huge presence like this, you keep other people around you small. They do not have power or anything attention-worthy. You always dwarf them. Not only is this unpleasant for people, but it makes them feel like they are inferior to you.

Playing the Victim

Playing the victim helps you appear innocent. If someone confronts you for doing something wrong, you can pretend that you are the real victim in the situation and that you were only behaving in a certain way to defend yourself. Spin things so that the other person looks guilty.

Playing the victim also gets people to feel sorry for you. People are more likely to take care of you and help you when they think that you have been wrongfully hurt. If you appear like the victim, people will defend you and they will not suspect you for any wrongdoing.

Unfortunately, playing the victim is a well-known manipulation tactic. Many people will not tolerate it. If you play the victim too often, you may just find that this tactic stops working for you. Whip out the victim act only when you have no other options. Never abuse it.

Use VAKOG

VAKOG stands for Visual, Auditory, Kinesthetic, Olfactory, and Gustatory. These are all five of the human senses. You want to use all of them to influence people and manipulate them. Expose a person to all of the senses to work successful manipulation.

If you want someone to go to a certain restaurant with you, let him smell food. If you want someone to get you a certain gift, drop hints about it and subtly make sure that he sees ads or pictures of the item you desire. Leave a catalog out open to a picture of a diamond ring if you are a girlfriend seeking a ring for Christmas, for instance.

Modeling

To get someone to do something for you or to be a certain way around you, you must create a model. You can be the model yourself or you can point out another person who is exhibiting the ideal behavior. People who love you will follow your lead in order to please you and establish rapport with you.

For example, if you want someone to lose weight, you can use the model of being thin and fit yourself. You can also point out other people and say, "She's so thin. I find that so attractive." You can simultaneously hurt someone and manipulate him or her to lose weight this way.

Chapter 5: Persuasion

Persuasion and manipulation often go hand in hand. Manipulation is often the act of subtly persuading someone to do your bidding. However, not all persuasion uses manipulation. Persuasion can be blatant, or it can call for a level of subtle influence on par with manipulation. While manipulation is almost always considered negative, persuasion can be used for either good or bad ends.

Learning how to persuade people can help you tremendously in psychological warfare. You can convince people to support you and be your ally. You can convince people to hate your enemy. You can persuade your enemy to trust you so that you can swoop in and betray him, as Sun Tzu preaches in the Thirty-Six Strategies I went over before. Finally, you can persuade anyone to do what you want so that you have the ultimate power. Persuasion can give you the ability to change your life for the best. That is one of the uses of psychological warfare, to get your way in order to improve your life as you see fit.

Cialdini's Six Influences

Dr. Robert Cialdini came up with six principles of persuasion. He wrote about them in his 1984 book *Influence.* These are foolhardy ways to influence other people. They are very necessary to influence people to do what you want. You can apply these principles to the persuasion aspects of psychological warfare.

Reciprocity

Reciprocity calls on someone's obligation to repay you in some way. It draws on the principle that people are never altruistic. If you do something for someone, then they are more likely to return the favor somehow. Therefore, you want to present yourself as a generous person. Always be performing favors and kind gestures for people. People will thus feel indebted to you and will strive to repay you.

This is why businesses offer free candy or customer appreciation days. The belief is that by doing something nice, they make their customers want to do business with them. You can do this too by jumping at any chance to do someone a favor so that you have many people wanting to help you. Being a helpful, kind person by reputation will earn you a great deal of help from others.

Consistency and Commitment

People respond best to things that are aligned with their personal beliefs and values. They value consistency in life and they will commit to something if it is consistent with their beliefs. Learn as much as you can about people in order to find out how you can spin something you want to fit one of their personal values.

For instance, if someone loves animals, then he is likely to support animal-related causes. Therefore, if you want him to support a cause for you, spin it so that it seems to benefit animals. He will be more likely to donate to your cause.

You can also play on someone's commitment to something. For instance, people will have more faith in their own children to do well in school. You can use this to your advantage by flattering them and saying, "I know your children will do well in school."

Social Proof

The fact that humans are social animals means that people are more likely to do what everyone else is doing. This is why trends take off. People are essentially copycats without meaning to be. You can persuade people to do something if you can make them think that everyone else will be doing it, too. You can also convince people that they can be trendsetters by doing something that is sure to catch on.

Use the idea that something is preferred, as well. If you say that other people prefer your product or idea over others, then people are more likely to want to do what you say. They figure that if other people like what you are offering, then they will too.

One way to use social proof to your favor is to make generalizations. Say things like, "Everyone is doing this" or "Everyone loves this." These generalizations create the illusion that the majority is doing something. People will be inclined to follow suit.

Liking

You can influence people that like you. People who like you want to please you. They are more likely to do things for you, to believe what you say, and to buy the things that you are selling.

Getting people to like you is the hard part. By being a good listener, people will love you. People love to talk so listen and ask involved questions to convey your great interest. People will come to admire you as a great listener and a great person.

Another way to use liking to your advantage is to make it appear like you have many friends already. If you seem popular, other people will want to join the party. People are driven by a herd instinct and will do what everyone else does. If everyone seems to like you, or you make it seem like everyone does, then people will feel the need to like you. Pretend to always be on your phone with countless contacts and drop countless names to make yourself appear to be the most popular person in the world.

Authority

Having authority means that people will listen to you and obey you. You want to project authority to persuade people to do what you are asking. People will follow your lead without question if you seem like an expert. Just pretending to be an authority will have surprising success. If your opinions are strong and you believe in your own expertise, you can convince others to do the same.

One way to use authority is to set a trend. You can influence other people to do what you want by first doing it yourself. If you are a great authority, people will follow suit. Make what you are doing seem fun or somehow beneficial.

The other way is to convince people that you are right. Tell people what you believe in or what you want them to do. They will follow your lead if you seem like a true authority figure. They will take your word for it.

How can you seem like an authority figure? One way is to be very confident. Talk like you are an expert and never show doubt. Also, carry yourself in a power posture. A power posture calls for you to hold your head high and your shoulders back, with your chest out. You will appear like a force to be reckoned with this way. If you really want to seem like an authority, research your topic of influence well so that you know what you are talking about. Endorsements, certificates, and awards are great ways to show off your excellence and authority in a field.

People are more likely to listen to you or buy your product if you are a verifiable expert in a field. In psychological warfare, people are more likely to trust your judgment and follow what you say as you lead into harm's way.

Scarcity

You can drive someone to act by convincing him that something you offer will not be available for long or is very rare. People are naturally competitive animals, and they will scramble to get resources that they think are about to be scarce. Therefore, when persuading someone, make it appear that resources are running low and this hot item will not be there for long. Someone is more likely to act in a hurry rather than take a long time to ponder the pros and cons.

Use scarcity to turn people against each other. "I had another gentleman express interest so you better act fast," is an example of something you might say to drive people to act in a hurry.

In psychological warfare, you can use the concept of scarcity to convince people to buy into your hype. If you are spreading political propaganda, for example, claim that time is running out. This will create panic and it will make people believe what you say with more urgency.

Body Language

It is believed that people communicate seven percent with words, and ninety-three percent with nonverbal communication. Nonverbal communication is the most crucial aspect of communication between people. It includes tone, facial expression, hand and body movement, and posturing, among other things. There is so much information contained in what people do with their bodies and facial explanations - far more than in what they explicitly say. As a result, you can use your body language to send subtle messages to other people, which is helpful in making yourself seem convincing. You want your body language to be warm, friendly, trustworthy, and above all consistent. Consistency helps people trust you and feel like your intentions are sincere.

Powerful Postures

Always have a powerful posture. This makes you seem confident and trustworthy. Other people will respond to you better. A powerful posture involves making yourself appear as tall as possible. Hold your head up, keep your spine ramrod straight, and thrust your chest and hips out before you wherever you walk.

Touching

Use light touching on someone's arm or hand to convey your sincerity and your friendliness. Light touching can make people feel close to you. Waitresses can actually get bigger tips by touching someone's hand when giving back change. Use this in conversation to convince someone of your closeness.

Do not use touching on people who are superior to you in hierarchy or rank. Touching can be viewed as a sign of disrespect. Also, stop using it if it appears to make someone uncomfortable. Heavy touching is inappropriate and will creep people out rather than get them to feel close to you. Most people respond well to light touching, however.

Proxemics

Proxemics is the study of how human beings use the space around them. Many people use the term "bubble" to describe their personal space. Never invade someone's bubble. To appear warm and ingratiating, you want to use space carefully. Try to keep a friendly space without getting too close. Generally, try to use public space at first and then move closer. Only move closer into someone's personal space if they invite you. Here are the different types of space:

Public space is usually twelve to twenty-five feet away from a person. This distance is the appropriate distance to keep away from utter strangers. An apology is in order if you accidentally are forced to enter this public space, such as on a crowded subway or bus. People can become extremely uncomfortable when their public space is violated by people that they do not know well, and they will likely either move away or grow suspicious and defensive.

Social distance is a little bit closer, four to twelve feet. This is the space that people use when interacting with acquaintances, such as work colleagues. It is also an acceptable distance to use when trying to build a bond with someone for the purposes of stealth persuasion.

Personal distance is the distance that people keep from good friends and family. Usually one must be invited into this space. You cannot just enter it without invitation if you are not close to someone.

Intimate distance is exclusively used for intimate exchanges, such as sex, kissing, hugging, or whispering secrets. Encroaching on intimate space can be very upsetting for people when they have not invited you into it.

Nodding

Nodding communicates that you are paying attention and really listening. It shows subtle and polite agreement. People like this, so they will respond you to more positively when you nod while talking to them. During conversation, nod in agreement often to establish a sense of closeness and connection. This will help you ingratiate yourself to a person.

Nod frequently throughout conversation. Even nod when you are not required to say yes. This gives others the impression that you connect deeply with what they are saying and that you understand and even empathize. People like this and they will come to trust you more.

Mirroring

When two people like one another, they often mirror one another's subtle movements. They sit leaning toward each other and copy similar movements, such as laying their hands down on the table. When talking to someone, make it seem like you like them by mirroring their movements. Wait two to three seconds until after someone moves to copy the movement.

Eye Contact

Eye contact is so important when persuading someone. You can persuade someone to trust you and even want to help you by maintaining eye contact. Putting a little bit of vulnerable emotion into your eyes can help you appear more human, as well, which can appeal to others' sympathy and desire to help.

The only time when direct eye contact can pose a problem is between two alpha males or even alpha females. Two powerful people who sustain direct eye contact may see it as a challenge for power. Only one person can win. Avoid putting yourself in situations such as this, where you stand to enrage or else lose to someone who values their power.

Vocal Inflections

A vocal inflection is the speed and pitch of your voice. You raise your voice at the end of questions, and increase its volume at the end of exclamations. When you want to persuade someone of the urgency of something, use rapid speech to give the sense that rapid action is required. When you want to make something sound relaxing or wonderful, use slower speech. Your speech will work to influence the emotions that other people respond to you with.

Subliminal Tactics

Certain subliminal tactics can subtly influence someone's response to you. You do not have to say anything; the subliminal tactics work for you. These are sneaky tactics that many politicians and salespeople use to gain control over others. They can easily help you in psychological warfare because they allow you to silently and cleverly manipulate the ways other people respond to you.

Presuppositions

Tell someone how he feels using presuppositions. If done correctly, you will convince someone to feel a certain way based on what you say. You can say things like, "You are going to love this...." Or "You will really want this because it will make you feel better." Use presuppositions to convince someone that you know how he feels and he will likely believe you and become persuaded.

Write Things Down

While someone is talking, grab a pen and paper and begin taking notes. Nothing is more successful at making people feel that their opinions matter. You can convince someone that you have his ultimate best interests at heart when you jot down everything that he says. Use this to help him overcome any objections that he may have to whatever you are trying to persuade him about.

Framing

Framing involves phrasing your words in such a way that people are logically driven to give the response you desire. Rather than focusing on changing the main point, it is possible to change the frame, or the context, of what you are saying. That allows for persuasion.

There are three elements to framing: placement, approach, and word choice. Placement is connecting with people at the right time. Approach people when they are tired, or scared by a recent event such as a terrorist attack. At these vulnerable times, people are more open to saying yes to change and to taking action that they view as helpful.

Approach involves appealing to people by offering either a positive gain or loss that they will get from doing what you want. For instance, a weight loss ad's approach is convincing people to buy a weight loss product because of the loss it promises. A gym can approach people by offering weight loss as well as the gain of confidence, attractiveness, and muscle tone.

Word choice is also a sneaky and important aspect of framing. The way words are strung together can have a positive or negative effect on the listener. Always use word combinations that evoke positive images in the person you are attempting to persuade. Make things sound good and upbeat, not bad and stressful.

Contrast Framing

Contrast framing is shifting someone's focus away from the negative and onto the positive. Make someone feel like the cons are far outweighed by the pros of making a decision.

For instance, if someone does not want to buy something from you because it is too pricey, take his mind off of the price tag and direct it instead to how he will benefit from owning the item. "You can't live without it. Your life will improve exponentially," you may say.

Physical Framing

Just as framing lets you frame your words in a certain context, physical framing allows you to create a physical setting for your words. A physical setting can help put the person you are persuading into a certain frame of mind. It can put them in the mood necessary for them to say yes.

If you want a woman to say yes to you when you propose to her for marriage, then put her in a physical frame of romantic intimacy. This is why men often propose in swanky restaurants, with classical music and candlelight. If you want someone to help you fix up your house, put them inside your house and show him how awful your living conditions are. When selling a house, realtors often bake cookies to make it seem more like a home atmosphere to potential buyers.

Reframing

Reframing someone's emotions to make him more positive and excited about doing something for you. Reframing calls for changing someone's view of a situation. It is the opposite of framing. Often, you will need to reframe someone's negative mood into a positive one. However, you can reframe emotions into whatever behooves you for persuasion to take place.

If someone gripes about working later, reframe his mood to happiness by reminding him that working late will put him on the big boss's good side. "There might be a raise in your future," you can say meaningfully.

Ask Yes Questions

The more people start saying yes, the more likely they are to keep saying yes. Ask people lots of questions with sure yes answers, to put them into the frame of mind where they say yes a lot. Then, they are more likely to say yes when you ask them for a favor or to buy something.

Getting people to say yes to you is easy if you start with small things, such as, "The weather sure is nice, isn't it?" Also called creating a yes-set, you can get someone into a positive frame of mind by creating a strong yes-set.

One way to create a yes-set involves asking tag questions. These are questions where you throw "tags" such as "right?" or "don't you think?" or "see?" in at the end of the question. People will naturally say yes to these tag questions. Lower their defenses and create a yes-set with special tag questions related to the subject that you are trying to persuade someone about.

Congruence

Congruence uses physical action to make people feel subconsciously pressured into saying yes. Using congruence requires you to stand your ground. You can push someone into action or a decision that you want using physical movements of motion.

If you are making a business deal, make it seem like saying no is not an option. Shake hands even before the deal is sealed. Or, if you are convincing your friend to come to a party, start walking toward the party as you two debate what you will be doing for the night. Walking in the direction of the party makes people feel like there is no point arguing because you are already on your way.

Fluid Speech

Having fluid speech means that you speak confidently. You are sure of what you are saying, so you do not stammer or stutter. Your words flow out of your mouth like fluid. Use fluid speech to appear knowledgeable and confident. People will recognize your authority and trust in your judgment. They will do your bidding as a result.

You should also gain elocution and enunciation to make your words very clear. Learn more words so that you can expand your vocabulary and seem more intelligent. This will make you appear like more of an authority, which is part of how you can convince people to do anything that you say.

Get People to Come to Conclusions Themselves

Instead of forcing your beliefs on someone, get them to come around to your logic. Then, he will think that the idea was his all along and he will accept it without resistance. Forcing your beliefs on people only encourages people to become resistant. Letting them come to conclusions on their own makes them feel in control.

Consider this example. You make a generalized statement, something such as, "If you don't study, you'll never get into college." A statement like this leaves an opening for the other person to respond with an exception, such as, "Dad never studied and he's an engineer." Another example is telling someone, "You need to go to bed or your growth will be stunted!" They can easily just counter your statement by telling you how someone they know is a night owl and the tallest person in class.

Instead of making a disputable blanket statement, tailor a question to the person's unique situation. "How do you think you will do on your test if you don't study? Do you think you'll be able to get into that college you wanted?" Or "Do you think it's healthy to get so little sleep?" The person will come to a conclusion himself.

Increments

I already discussed this in the chapter in manipulation. Keep it in mind when you are persuading someone of something. By introducing him to the idea in segments, or increments, you can make him feel more comfortable with the idea. He will slowly warm up to it and accept it.

Ask for Help

Asking a person for help makes a person feel helpful and needed. This is flattering, so he is likely to say yes. He is now ingratiated to you because he feels that he can help you. Once you have asked for help, you can begin asking him for other favors. This will subtly persuade him to want to be on your side and to help as much as possible. He will want to preserve his favor with you, since it makes his own ego feel good.

Women especially have luck with this trick. Try using a higher pitched voice if you are a woman to get men to help you. Men will very rarely say no.

Foot in the Door

You can get your foot in the door and increase your chances of getting a yes by asking someone for a small favor. Human beings are social creatures and hate saying no. If a small favor does not inconvenience someone, then he is very likely to say yes and do something small for you. He will have no qualms about helping you.

Then, you can later ask for a larger favor. A person is less likely to say no if he has already told you yes. You already have your foot in the door since he has already done something for you.

An example of this would be asking someone to help you carry a heavy box up to your apartment. Once in the apartment, ask for a larger favor, such as to help you move the rest of your stuff in.

Offer a Warm Drink

To persuade people, you want to appear warm. You want people to think that by pleasing you, they are doing something good. Convincing people that you are a warm and loving person can get people to feel like they want to help you by doing things for you. Imagine a warm professor, inviting students into his office for chats by the fire. This professor exudes warmth and his students become eager to please him.

One easy trick to get people to subconsciously believe that you are warm and likable is to ply them with a warm drink. For some reason, people are prone to associate the warm drink between their palms with you. They come to think of you as a warm and inviting person who cares about their well-being. They will thus warm up to you, and they will be more likely to do what you want.

Overcome Objections

Think of all the possible objections someone could have to your proposal. When you later try to persuade him, you can hit all the points that he is likely to object to. This can help him feel comfortable saying yes to you, since it will appear that you have already addressed all of his possible concerns.

Do not even let someone raise objections to you. Counter objections before a person even has a chance to mention them. If someone is able to voice his own fears, those fears will become more real to him. Prevent him from making his fears real by addressing them first and dismissing them.

Chapter 6: The Importance of Deception

You must become adept at deception to use psychological warfare. Psychological warfare is deceptive by nature. It also calls for the use of deception with victims and others in order to create the atmosphere that is conducive to mental control and harm.

Many people are adept at deception already. Deception starts early in childhood and is a part of one's personality by the age of ten, psychologists estimate. Even babies lie when they cry for milk, but really they just want attention. That means that you already know how to lie and you likely have many times throughout your life. But are you a good liar? Or do you give yourself away and get your stories confused? If so, you need to greatly improve your deception skills to be a good liar. You cannot be running psychological warfare on people while giving away that you have nefarious motives.

Deception is very useful in psychological warfare. When you are trying to convince people to believe something that is a lie, you must create an infallible and believable façade, or fake reality of sorts, that people can and will believe. This reality takes effort and skill to create and maintain. You may show people this reality through propaganda or some other form of media. You can convince them of this reality's truthfulness by being a very thoroughly convincing liar. You must never let the façade drop, or you will lose control over your victims.

In addition, you want to use deception well when you are smearing someone's reputation and discrediting them. As you learned earlier, this is an essential step in psychological warfare. It is a way to incapacitate people from being believable when they try to confront you for any sort of mischief. It also makes people feel like their sanity is questionable, which disables their trust in themselves.

Moreover, you can protect yourself from being caught with deception. Lie through your teeth if you have to. But you never want to get caught.

In the following pages, you will find some tips for lying well. The main tip that you need to follow is removing all inconsistent behavior that makes your behavior stand out while you are telling a lie. If you can do this, then you can really avoid giving yourself away and arousing suspicion.

Be Consistent

This is the cardinal rule to lying. If you act inconsistent in your behavior, you give away your dishonesty. If your words do not match the emotions in your face and body language, then you raise others' suspicions. You also must maintain consistency in the details of your stories so that you do not give away the fact that you are lying with a changing story.

When you lie, you must try to act like you always do to avoid setting off alarm bells for people who know you well. You must maintain consistency in behavior while you lie as well. Make sure that you look sad if your story is sad. Keep your posture and body language relaxed and natural. Make sure that your stories remain consistent. Consistency is easy when you believe your lie and when you believe that you are doing nothing wrong. Keeping the details of your story at a minimum is also helpful so that you can remember your lie and keep it the same.

Plan Your Lie

Lies that are well-planned usually are more convincing, psychologists say. Lies require you to jump over some ethical hurdles and struggle as you think of what to say. Therefore, planning a lie removes the need to struggle in creating a story. You will seem more polished and believable.

First, use your time to create alibis if you can. Set up a routine. Get people to lie for you.

Take the time you need to fabricate a wonderfully convincing lie with a solid background.

Second, think of a great and convincing story. Then stick to that story, no matter what. You can find ways to defend your story if you stand by it. Be sure that your story is logical and believable, and also make sure that you do not create too many details. However, you can create more details if you are pressed.

Third, think of a fallback option should you ever get caught. This could be the truth. It could be another lie. Whatever you do, you want to have an explanation for why you lied. You could say that you simply forgot something, or you could admit to lying. You should create several fallback options that are suitable for a variety of outcomes of your initial lie.

Follow Conversational Rules

When using deception, you want to appear as normal as possible. One way to do this is to follow all of the rules that govern normal conversation. These rules are rules that we inadvertently follow when communicating with others. These rules keep communication clear.

The first rule is the maxim of quality. This is where people expect you to provide honest answers. You can take advantage of this by expecting people to believe you. This expectation works because it makes you appear more confident. You can react to disbelief with indignance, to make people feel like they were wrong for doubting you.

The second is the maxim of quantity. People expect you to reveal a normal level of detail, not too little or too much. For instance, you do not want to answer questions about your day by gabbing away with all the details or just saying, "Not much."

The third rule is the maxim of relation, which means that you stay on topics that are related to your original conversation topic.

Abruptly changing the subject is suspicious and abnormal.

The final rule involves the maxim of manner, which means that your answers should be direct and to the point. If someone asks you how they look, they want a phrase like, "You look good." Saying that someone looks interesting can be confusing because it is not direct, and that implies that you might be thinking something bad.

Always follow these maxims when you speak with others to avoid arousing suspicion. Your conversation will seem normal and rhythmed, and people will not suspect you of lying when you seem normal. You never want to talk too little or too much, use unclear phrases, change the subject abruptly, or provide obviously erroneous answers. If you violate any of these conversational rules, you can arouse a lot of suspicion about your honesty and the motives lying underneath your conversation.

You can flip these conversational maxims to mislead people. You can use the maxim of relations to change the subject, giving the hint that you do not want to follow the line of conversation anymore. This subject change can imply to people that you are not willing to discuss the matter anymore. This can prevent them from digging further and learning the real truth.

You can also use the maxim of quantity to tell a lie by omission. You give just enough information that it makes your conversation partner feel like you are telling the truth. But you leave out something. While this is technically lying, you can also claim, "I forgot" or "I didn't think it was important" if your omission is ever found out.

You should avoid telling bold-faced lies unless you know that your false story can never be verified as a lie. When you do tell a lie, it is best to gloss over it and include as few details as possible. But tell enough details that it seems convincing and not suspicious.

Obscure Details

When using deception, it is best to be vague about the details. The fewer details you mention, the fewer things you need to keep track of in order to keep your stories straight. You then run less of a risk of giving yourself away by messing up a tiny detail later on. People often forget small details, but you will be surprised what people can remember, especially if they suspect you of lying. You never want to give someone any little thing that they can remember and use against you later on.

You also have less to come up with while fabricating a falsehood. This can make lying easier. Just focus on creating the bare bones details and then moving on. You can blame incorrect or left-out details on your faulty memory if need be.

Body Language

Your body language can give you away, so keep your body language as truthful and consistent as possible. You can give away that something is off or different if you have unnatural, stiff body language or shifty eye contact. Alternatively, leaning too far forward or holding eye contact too much is also suspicious. The best way to act is to act like you are doing nothing wrong.

This is where imagining that you are innocent, whether you really are or not, is extremely helpful. If you really think that you are innocent, then your body language will reflect your innocence. You want to appear relaxed when you are lying. You will not betray any tells because you are not feeling nervous and guilty.

Specifically, you want to avoid grooming yourself, rubbing your hands together, fidgeting, or licking your lips. You want to also avoid turning a shoulder to the person you are lying to or avoiding eye contact with them. If you are sweaty out of nervousness, do not give it away by wiping frantically at your sweat. Keep your shoulders relaxed, keep your hands on the table in front of you or at your sides, and maintain normal eye contact.

Use Affection and Physical Closeness

When you are lying to loved ones, maintaining affection and physical closeness are great ways to give the appearance of honesty. You can seem trustworthy if you are affectionate. Offer reassuring touch and hugs to your loved ones as you lie, and do everything you can to ingratiate yourself with them.

You do not want to do this in a way that is inconsistent with your normal behavior. As I said before, consistency is crucial to avoid arousing suspicion.

This can also work in the form of flirting with cops or other officials. Showing affection and desire can sway authority figures from taking harsh action on you. This will charm authorities, and they will be more likely to believe you and want to help you. They will not want to believe that you are lying.

Don't Wait to Be Asked

Volunteer information right away without waiting to be asked. This will make you seem like you are being upfront. It also gives you the momentum to create and perpetuate a lie. Hesitation is not favorable when lying. It makes you look less believable.

Lie to Yourself

You probably already lie to yourself to a degree. Humans are masters at self-deception. When confronted with a truth that you are not comfortable with, you may distort this truth totally. You may repress memories and emotions. This self-deception protects your mind from harm. While it is not always effective at healing your mental wounds, it can be very useful in the art of deception.

Psychologists say that people who engage in self-deception are overall better liars. Pathological liars are the best at quickly and shamelessly convincing themselves that their lies are true.

You can convince yourself of the truth of a lie that you are telling. When you at least partially believe the lie, you are more likely to indicate that with your body language and speech. Therefore, you become more convincing and you calm down your nervous tells.

Avoid Lying Too Much

Avoid lying too much. In other words, have a purpose for lying. Lie only when it is absolutely imperative. Make sure that you have a good reason to lie and then put all of your effort in that lie. Lie when your reputation or your life depends on it.

Try to build a reputation as a solid, honest person. This will make you more credible. People will think that you are trustworthy. Once you have earned everyone's trust, it is easier to get away with the occasional necessary lie. Lying all the time makes you sloppy, and you will get caught. You will become less trustworthy.

You will find that honesty really is the best policy most of the time. Sometimes, you feel scared and tempted to lie. You think that someone will have a severe reaction. However, you cannot read minds and you may just be surprised at how well people will handle the truth. By telling the truth more often than not, you remove the stress of having to come up with likely stories and keeping them straight. In addition, you make your lies more believable when you do tell them.

Mix in Some Truth

The very best lies are hard to catch because they contain bits of truth. Truthful details can serve you well because they can mislead people from suspecting or disbelieving the dishonesty that you have also uttered.

Make sure that your lie is at least fifty percent truth. Add in as many truthful details as possible. This will make your lie seem honest.

You can also lie by omission. Tell the truth, but omit a few details. If someone confronts you about lying, just claim, "I didn't lie. I just forgot to mention that." It is even better to use manipulation and claim, "I didn't lie. You just didn't ask." Make it seem like someone else's fault.

Include Normal Details

Always include the normal amount of detail. Too much detail makes your lie harder to verify, but too little makes it seem like you are hiding something. Think about how much detail you would normally include. Stick to that.

Put Pressure on Someone

You can put pressure on people to get them to believe you. By putting pressure on somebody, you can take away their ability to discern if you are lying or telling the truth. Hurry someone along or act irritable when they question you.

There are many ways to put pressure on someone. You can use guilt and remind people of all the nice things you have done for them in the past. "Why would you think I am lying to you? After all I have done for you?"

You can use accusations, which are covered in greater depth in a few sections. You can even say that you are running out of time or that you do not have time for their accusations. The sense of urgency is the best way to ramp up the pressure.

Know Your Tells and Avoid Them

All liars have tells. The human mind must struggle to think of a story. Lies require more mental effort than the truth does, since you must fabricate a story. Therefore, you often pause or engage in other activities as your mind races to fill in the blanks. In addition, you may be nervous and this may make you act in weird little ways.

Everyone has their own special tell. Yours may include playing with your hair, biting your lip, shaking or flexing your foot, picking at your nails, organizing the clutter on the table, or straightening your tie or other articles of clothing. Organizing and cleaning are common tells because they represent how you are trying to organize a lie in your mind.

Avoid excessive grooming, fidgeting, or other nervous behaviors. Also avoid looking guilty by avoiding eye contact. Maintain normal eye contact and a relaxed posture. If you become sweaty, don't wipe at your forehead to get away the sweat. Wiping off your face and neck is another big tell. Just let the sweat gather there and try to relax. This can calm your nerves and stop the sweating.

Bargain

In the event that you are caught lying, you want to remove your guilt through a process known as bargaining. You put distance between yourself and a lie. You make it seem like you are justified for lying, or that your guilt is minimal. You convince other people that they have no right to be angry with you for your deception.

One way to do this is to make it seem like it's the victim's fault that you lied. "I had no choice to lie to you because you are so unreasonable and never understanding," you might say. Do everything to make the victim seem guilty, rather than you. This is manipulation and it works.

You can also make it seem like the lie is really not that big of a deal. "So what, I lied? Everybody does." Remove someone's right to feel angry or hurt by making it seem like their emotions are unreasonably harsh and dramatic for the occasion.

The best weapon you can use in this case is to point out what someone else did wrong.

This detracts attention away from you and what you did wrong. It makes the victim seem like he or she is somehow in the wrong. As he becomes defensive, he will stop focusing on the lie and instead will focus on sticking up for himself. You can bring up past issues or other issues instead of the lie. Bring up upsetting things that will make your victim feel guilty.

Counterattack

Accuse other people of lying or other wrongdoing when they accuse you. Counterattacking is a special favorite with politicians and lawyers. Instead of taking the blame for your own lie, shift the focus off of yourself and onto others. Make others feel guilty and defensive, and discredit their reputations. No one has the right to accuse you of anything, so do not allow it.

When someone begins to claim that you are a liar, just turn the accusation back onto them. Better yet, accuse them of bigger lies or other wrongs that they have committed in the past. Attack them in a way that is far worse than the way that they are attacking you.

Tell People what They Want to Hear

People are selective listeners. This means that they only hear what they want to. You can tell people lies and let them pick out the details that they are bound to like. Details that boost their egos are sure to work.

Later, if someone confronts you, you can say that they only heard part of what you said. Convince him that he was selectively listening. You can even get angry and claim that he was not listening to you at all.

Know when You're in too Deep

It is possible to get in too deep. You know that you cannot keep the lie up. You have two options: change your lie or tell the truth. Which option you should take is entirely dependent on the situation. Usually, telling the truth is best.

Lying can be very stressful. It can tear down your relationships. Therefore, you should only lie when it helps you. You should not bother to keep up a lie that is causing you more trouble than good. That defeats the whole purpose of good deception.

However, in psychological warfare, part of the purpose of lying is to mess with someone's perception of the world. If you are in too deep, you can always add more lies. Or claim that you never said what you did when you lied. This is a form of gaslighting. It will cause your victim to start to question his sanity. In this case, continuing to lie is preferable to telling the truth.

Chapter 7: Attitude

Attitude drives psychological warfare. By having a certain attitude, you master yourself and you master your enemy. You can project confidence and the image that you are doing nothing wrong. This will subdue your enemy and help you win. You want to exude the aura of authority and you want to be intimidating as well.

Have the attitude that you have already won. This cockiness is a good way to disarm and weaken enemies. If you convey the attitude that you have already won, people are more likely to accept this with resignation and to not challenge you. Your attitude of being right is an authority attitude. Most people will bow down and respect authority. Those who challenge authority often will not keep doing so if you assert your authority strongly.

Have confidence. If you are insecure or unsure of yourself, you appear weak. Other people will believe that they have a chance to beat you or overcome your psychological warfare if you come off as weak. Make an impression of strength.

Really, you want to be intimidating. The best way to appear intimidating is to tower over other people. Try to stand as tall as you can. Also flex your muscles and even build muscles so that you appear large. Largeness is what intimidates others. Aggressive body language, such as crossed arms, finger shaking, and close physical proximity, can be used to achieve the desired intimidating effect as well. Never smile; instead, scowl. Angry and ugly facial expressions can make you intimidating as well.

Passive aggressive speech and behavior can also make you intimidating. You can appear friendly, but then you drop hints that you are not happy. You can say things like, "Sure I will help you. I always help everyone and no one helps me. Oh well." By pretending to be friendly, you can convey your aggression without being called on it.

Always believe that you are doing nothing wrong. Everything you do has a justifiable reason. There is a reason that you are committed to what you are doing. Allowing guilt, doubt, or regret to creep into your attitude gives your enemy a foothold. You do not want to do this. Just keep remembering your motivation if you feel like are beginning to reconsider your position.

Look at how threatening leaders in the world behave. The most evil dictators and classic James Bond villains are often charming, aloof, and somewhat distant. They are fascinating people. They do not reveal much about themselves or their plans. But they also have large egos and believe that they will win and that they are in the right. These cool, aloof people are charismatic and chillingly powerful leaders. This is because they emit an aura of authority that commands respect. You can emulate their natures to become respected and feared.

It is important to become very Machiavellian in your behavior and your view of the world. When you adopt more Machiavellian thought, you view people as pawns to be used to your advantage. You do not let remorse or pity get in the way of what you want. Other people are here to serve you and not to be served by you. With this attitude, you will have the ability to take advantage of people and to scan people for clues that you can later use against them to manipulate them. You will be a fearless and unstoppable leader who feels no guilt or remorse for anything.

Chapter 8: Specific Uses of Psychological Warfare

In the following chapter, we will discuss some more specific uses of psychological warfare that could greatly influence your personal life. While these examples are not all-inclusive, they can give you a foundation for applying the concepts contained in this book to real-life situations.

Love

Psychological warfare can help you out a great deal in love. You can get people to love you and do anything for you. You can score the man or woman of your dreams and you can manipulate your love partners into doing whatever you want. You can make people ingratiate themselves to you so that your ego can enjoy a nice boost. You can get people to lie for you and work hard for you if you ingratiate yourself to them enough.

Seduction

You can seduce anyone by offering them what they really want. If you want them and they want something else, offer them what they really want to get them to want you. Most people want love and ego gratification, so offer heaps of this to the person that you are trying to seduce. The person will come to associate you with feeling good, and he or she will want to stick around.

The key to seduction is making someone feel great around you. This gets love hormones flowing. Use flattery, flirting, and adoration. Give a person gifts and heaps of affection. Do things that get him or her blushing and flushed with hormones.

Also dress to impress. Hold your head high and show your pride. This confidence is sexy and seductive. Appear important, too. You can do this by making yourself look taller with shoes or posture, and by talking to people like you are someone to be respected. Importance will make people want to get to know you. The first introduction is the first step to getting into their heads and hearts.

Use flirtatious body language to make people aware of your interest. Angle your feet toward them. Lean forward and cup your head in your hand while they talk. Touch them lightly often. Try to facilitate physical closeness with your body.

Make lots of subliminal linguistic tricks. Use language that brings people around to the idea that they love you. "How long have you loved me?" is one example of a question that introduces the idea of love to people's brains. Also try to use more active words to encourage action. Instead of saying, "Would you like to go to dinner?" say, "Let's go to dinner now!"

Also, use the framing we talked about in the chapter on persuasion. Ask someone lots of questions with guaranteed yes answers. That way, they are in the habit of saying yes and they are more likely to agree to a date. You can also ask them to do something absurd, and when they say no, ask, "Well, OK, but would you go out on a date with me?" A date suddenly seems like a smaller commitment and they will be more likely to say yes.

Hide how bad things really are in your life. Act like everything is peachy. That way, people will associate you with positivity and they will have a better impression of you. Constantly complaining or demanding help can make you look pathetic and weak and not attractive.

Manipulation

You can easily manipulate people who are close to you because you know them well. You know how to make them tick and how to make them smile. You are already deeply involved in a person's life, so you are in the perfect position to use manipulation.

Women have a special advantage when manipulating men. Because men have a natural instinct to protect women, women can get men to do anything. Women should always use their highest pitched voices to motivate men. This signals their femininity and their need to be protected and provided for.

Watch for someone's weaknesses. Use that weakness to hook the person. You can use weaknesses to make someone so scared of you that they will do anything to escape the consequences of displeasing you, or you can make someone weak with desire for you. Threaten and offer good things all that you can. Create a confusing web of gratitude and fear around people to bind them to you. People will never leave you if they feel that they depend on you and that they will never be loved or wanted by anyone else.

Sex is always a good weapon. Sex can be used for control. You can use it to bribe and influence people. You can also use sex to make people feel horrible. If you make someone feel guilty or abandoned after having sex with you, you just manufactured a great sexual weapon.

You can also make your partner feel like everything is his or her fault, so that you are never to blame for anything. Should your partner accuse you of wrongdoing, twist the accusation onto him or her. "You made me act like this," you can say, to absolve yourself of all guilt.

Distorting what your partner says is another good way to make yourself seem like an innocent victim so that you never appear guilty of anything. It can also drive your partner crazy so that he or she begins to doubt his or her sanity, and turns to you for guidance on how to approach the world. Deliberately take everything someone says wrong. Accuse your partner of saying things that he or she did not mean. Make him or her feel like you are constantly being hurt, and that he or she is always in the wrong and can't even talk to you right.

Emotional Abuse

Emotional abuse is a good way to gain complete control over someone. Many emotional abusive behaviors reflect the same actions committed by the government to control its people. That is why emotional abuse can be considered a form of psychological warfare.

This form of abuse simply calls for the perpetuation of emotional pain in your partner in a way that prevents him or her from understanding that you are being abusive. He or she will always seem like the perpetrator, rather than the victim.

Discounting someone's emotions is a good place to start. Discounting involves making someone feel guilty or even stupid for having the feelings and reactions that one has. You can use eye rolls, bored sighs, and even jokes to discount someone's emotions. If someone accuses you of abuse, claim that he or she is just being oversensitive and needs to just get over it.

You can counter someone's perceptions and emotional experiences in order to limit someone's joy and confidence. For instance, if someone loves a certain food, counter it by saying, "That will make you fat." You thus ruin someone's favorite food while also suppressing his or her enjoyment of it.

Use harsh criticism to hurt someone's feelings. Make disparaging comments about a person's appearance and personality to lower his or her self-esteem. You can cripple a person's self-image and confidence with mean remarks. You can also make someone feel scared to do anything, out of fear that you will judge them harshly.

Undermine someone's thoughts and feelings by belittling them. You can make someone feel very unimportant this way. This hurts their feelings as well as their confidence.

Finally, you can insult someone openly. When he or she confronts you, say that you were only joking. Tell someone to get over it. "You are way too sensitive. I'm just being funny."

Punishment

Punish someone when he or she goes against your wishes. You can make someone afraid to displease you because he or she knows that terrible consequences await. Punishment should never have to include beating someone. It is far better to use psychological warfare to get your way. You can create such unpleasant situations for a loved one mentally that he or she will strive to please you for fear of the mental consequences.

Punish someone with the silent treatment. The silent treatment is a form of emotional abuse. This is because it involves withholding love from someone and making someone feel intensely uncomfortable. If you have suffered the silent treatment, then you know how uncomfortable it is. You feel scared to even breathe around someone who refuses to acknowledge you or meet your eyes. Offer the silent treatment whenever someone transgresses around you, and you will see that he or she is soon afraid of upsetting you and will tread on eggshells around you for fear of displeasing you.

You can forget the things that are important to someone as a form of punishment. Conveniently forget to pick up his or her favorite snack at the store, where you just bought everyone else's favorite snacks. People will learn to please you if they want their favorite things.

You can also use guilt to break someone down. Whenever problems arise in the relationship, shift the blame onto the other person. Punish him or her for everything that is wrong. Say things like, "You always do this," or "Nothing I do is enough for you." This guilt is punishment enough. It will quickly erode someone's confidence and convince someone that he or she is always wrong. He or she will strive to do better to avoid displeasing you and earning more of your disapproval.

Say things like, "Forget it," "Whatever," and "Never mind" to avoid arguments. This can make your partner feel shut out and guilty for the problems in the relationship.

Revenge

Psychological warfare has some potentially very harmful applications. It can be used for revenge so that you can satisfy your feelings of hurt and betrayal.

Use psychological warfare to convince someone that he is a horrible person. You can strip away his pride and his self-esteem through subliminal hints of his awfulness. In addition, you can turn people against him by spreading rumors about him and discrediting his reputation. You can break down everything that boosts his self-esteem.

You can use propaganda to make someone lose his job, his loved ones, and his good reputation. By breaking down everything he has, you will remove his will to live and his happiness. You will destroy him. It is a good idea to remove someone's supports in order to break his spirit and even remove his will to live.

You can also drive someone crazy, using the methods discussed earlier. Use such methods as gaslighting to make him question his sanity. It will drive him into a very uncomfortable place of doubt. Use the other forms of psychological torture that I went over in any way that you can in order to hurt him.

Monetary Success

In the world of business, manipulation is part of the game. You cannot get ahead with sheer honesty and sweetness. Sometimes, you have to be ruthless. You have to use whatever means necessary to get what you are after. The only way to make lots of money is to go after money ruthlessly and never let anything stop you.

Seem Important

You want to always seem important. This will make people look up to you. Take your job seriously, dress to impress, and speak to people as if they are your inferiors. Of course, you will want to treat your management and your clients as equals and address them with due respect to appeal to them. Walk around with an air that you own the place.

Associate with the strongest, most important people in the office. You are guilty by association. If you associate with weak subordinates, you will appear weak and inferior yourself. Having powerful associations makes you appear more powerful.

Alternatively, you should appeal to weak people to create a legion. Then, you can overthrow the top dogs in your business and achieve that coveted position for yourself. Sometimes, befriending the weak people is beneficial. Weak people are more likely to follow you and to ingratiate themselves to you. They are more likely to do whatever you ask them to in order to make you happy. They can be powerful allies.

Make Smart Decisions

Make smart decisions without any remorse or hesitation. If something seems like a good idea to you, do it. Do not let morals or the fear of risks stop you from anything at all. Even if your decisions are not optimal, you can treat them as such. Then other people will not question your judgment as much. This is why you need to approach life with an attitude of authority.

Intimidate Competition

Business calls for you to be cutthroat. Therefore, it is essential to know how to cut down your enemies psychologically. You can successfully destroy competition in your office or in your field by using psychological warfare on them. You can also use these psychological warfare tactics to get rid of an employee or co-worker that threatens you in any way in the office.

The first step to breaking down people in business is to be intimidating. Use an intimidating posture and exaggerated height to give you a psychological edge over others. Then use your ruthless reputation of unfailing and merciless authority to further intimidate people.

Log every conversation and gather data on employees that you do not care for. Flood them with criticism and unclear assignments so that they perform poorly at work. Overwork them so that they become overwhelmed and perform poorly. Also remove their quality of life by making them work too much. Make sure to target their confidence so that they do not believe in themselves. "You do poor work" is the message you want to send. These employees will begin to fail due to lack of confidence and the sense of being overwhelmed, and you will have plenty of excuses to get them fired or reassigned.

Use passive aggressive means to hurt your co-workers. Disable their confidence. Spread rumors about them to get the other co-workers to dislike them. Hide important files or spill coffee on their laptops so that they bomb important presentations. Tell people wrong deadlines or whisper rumors that management is not happy with them. Work will become harder for your co-workers and your efforts may just get them fired or drive them to quit. You want to make the work environment as unbearable as possible to get rid of co-workers you hate.

Make sure to spread gossip and circulate bad publicity to undermine someone's reputation. This is especially useful when you are trying to undermine a competitor who is selling the same product as you. Discredit your competitor so that you appear like the superior seller.

Also be sure to twist the words of others in business. Use any little utterance from someone, take it out of context, and have a field day with it. This is how you can destroy business relationships and reputations.

Self-Improvement

Self-improvement is often hard. You can find yourself to be your own enemy in self-improvement. You can use psychological warfare to recreate yourself as you see fit by battering down your own resistance barriers to better habits. You can also use it to shape the people around you in order to gain the power needed for self-improvement. By manipulating other people to not smoke around you or to go work out with you, you can successfully alter your environment to become more conducive to your success in self-improvement.

You can also use psychological warfare methods on yourself. You can start to trick your brain into doing what you want it to do. Trick your brain into letting you lose weight, become smarter, and become more confident. One way you can do this is by using NLP modeling on yourself. Another way is by using persuasion tactics, such as framing, to make your mind think that taking certain action, such as working out, is a good idea.

Decide what you wish to improve about yourself. Then find out how you can persuade yourself to embrace your new habits.

Chapter 9: How to Protect Yourself

So far, this book has focused on teaching you how to inflict successful psychological warfare on others. Now I will show you what to do if this warfare is inflicted upon you. Psychological warfare is out there and it is real. You may just find yourself a victim at some point in life. It is very likely that you have already been a victim without even realizing it. After reading this book, you may become aware of psychological warfare attempts that have been made on you. You are not defenseless. Awareness is the first step to victory.

Who are potential abusers? They may be neighbors, exes, or even family. Anyone who has an agenda against you may be trying to run your life and influence your actions unfavorably. If you feel like a victim, then you probably are.

Look around your life. Are there things that happen to you that make no sense? Do people seem to avoid you for no reason, especially when they did not in the past? Do you find it hard to get a job? Do you find yourself acting or feeling in ways that make no sense? Do you find that your views on certain issues are shifting against your will and you believe things that you never used to without sufficient reason to change your beliefs? Does anything else in your life appear to have changed significantly for no discernible reason?

If you encounter any of these signs, you may just be a victim yourself. Understanding how to perform psychological warfare on others helps you realize when it is being performed on you. Use this book as a reference guide for the signs and symptoms of psychological warfare.

There are many reasons that you could be a victim. It is very rare that you are the innocent victim of government experimentation. While that possibility always exists, it is far more likely and probable that you are the victim of someone psychotic in your own life. It is probably a person that you know well and have frequent encounters with. Think about people who make you feel uncomfortable or who seem to have ulterior motives with you. Consider people that you have wronged, or who at least perceive that you have wronged them somehow. These are likely the ones who wish you harm.

Prevent Psychological Warfare

Choose what you allow into your life. You do not need to give certain people or situations the time of day. You are very busy and your time is precious. You need to protect your energy, resources, and intellect by associating only with the positive. Being selective about the people that you associate with also helps you keep your reputation intact, so that you can preserve it in the event that your enemy attacks it.

You should also be selective about the media and information that you take in. Psychological warfare is usually very covert. If you take in lots of information, you raise your risk of exposure. Only choose a few reliable sources of news, and avoid listening to people that do not seem trustworthy. Do not believe everything that you read; question everything and perform your own research on even your most reliable sources of information and news.

Choose your relationships wisely. You really cannot trust anyone. Avoid trusting people. You never know what information they may glean about you to use against you. Even the smallest amount of contact can be used against you. As you have learned from employing psychological warfare, manipulative and emotionally abusive people are able to glean conversations for the tiniest clues about you. They then use this information later to hurt you in some way.

Always be wary of people who try to bait you or distract you. Usually, their actions are not innocent. What are they trying to distract you from? Why do they want your attention? By distracting you, they may be trying to give you a subliminal cue or they may be trying to control you through power of suggestion. Either way, they are trying to dominate and monopolize your time. Ignore them or politely but firmly tell them no when they demand your attention.

When people try to take power over you, they may begin by stating you have glaring flaws. They do this to lower your self-esteem and make you sensitive. You do not need to fall for this. Just change the conversation or suggest that they have the same flaw. If someone says you have a bad temper, for instance, you can grin and say, "I know! But at least I don't hold everything in like you do. It is actually much healthier to have a bad temper like mine. How is your project coming along, by the way?" This is called deflection and it works miracles.

Remove yourself from drama and conflict. Stonewalling people is better than arguing with them. When you argue with people, you fuel their anger and animosity. You add power to the fight. When you pull away and act like a stone wall, you become unreachable. You win through silence. You also avoid making the enemies that may eventually attempt to perform psychological warfare on you by using stonewalling.

Do not let the opinions or actions of others change you. It is a natural human instinct to want to mirror the behavior of others to earn social approval. But social approval is highly overrated. You will be much happier and much safer if you keep to yourself and do your own thing. Act the way you want to act. Be who you want to be. By not buying into the need for social approval, you lower your risk for falling victim to mass fads. People can be controlled through things like social proof and fads. If you are not one of the herd, then you can avoid falling into trends that are created for mass control by the government or some other untrustworthy agent. You can be more discerning and determine what is safe, rather than blindly following other people's leads.

Avoid all contact with enemies. Again, this is important because your enemies may be trying to get pertinent information from you. It is also important because your enemies may be trying to poison you with their negative vibes. They may even be performing psychological warfare on you. Limit the exposure to avoid any harm. You do not need to waste time with people who do not care about you.

Establish a good reputation. This makes it harder for your enemies to discredit you. When you begin to find that you are a victim, people are more likely to believe your claims and rally for you if you have a good reputation. You can create a good reputation by always being nice and kind to others. Always be honest so that you look like a good person with unfailing integrity. You want to be someone that other people like.

Protect Your Mind and Your Heart

Protect your mind and your heart; they are the main targets of psychological warfare, more so than your physical body. By overturning the fear and hurt that your psychological warmonger inflicts upon you, you essentially win the war. Fear and pain are the primary weapons of psychological warfare. They are aimed at the primary targets, your heart and your mind. The only way you can defeat psychological warfare is by blocking the fear and pain. If you can reverse the fear and pain back on your attacker, you are even more of a victor in a psychological war.

Avoid falling victim to the power of suggestion. If someone suggests that you have a flaw or that you should do something, understand that they are using the power of suggestion to make you believe a self-limiting belief. Someone is trying to plant a bad thought about yourself into your head. By believing what they say, you become a victim. But you can fight their beliefs by believing in yourself. Undermine self-limiting beliefs that others try to plant into your mind by suggesting an alternative truth.

For example, if someone tells you, "You won't have any friends in life because you are an awful person," suggest that they may be wrong. "Are you sure that I am a terrible person?" you could say. By doing this, you are avoiding an argument because you are not being defensive. But you are opening the possibility that the person is wrong and that another truth is out there. You lead your mind to doubting the veracity of what the person is suggesting.

Also, continue to hold positive beliefs about yourself. Think that you are a good person and that you are well-loved. Think that you are smart and capable. Think thoughts that build you up, rather than tear you down. When you do this, you give yourself power and deny others the ability to take control of your low self-esteem. You protect your mind from bad suggestions and your heart from the pain that these suggestions can cause if you believe them.

Search for your enemy's weaknesses. Psychological warfare is very successful and effective, but its use suggests that your enemy is too weak to actually attack you. He or she can only employ covert methods. For instance, when the Iranian hostage situation occurred, the fear caused by the act only masked the true weakness of the Iranians. The Iranians did not have the guns and other weapons to beat the US at war. Rather, they had to use fear and terrorism to achieve their goal of harming the US. Your attacker is probably instilling fear in you to mask his or her true weakness. Use your attacker's weakness as a means to overcome the fear that your attacker inspires in you. You are probably stronger than he or she is, if you just drop the fear and learn to believe in yourself. There is also probably nothing real to be scared of.

Likely, your attacker uses the power of intimidation. This power is great and it can make you cower in terror. But realize that intimidation is usually just a front that a scared bully erects for his or her own protection. Has your intimidator ever actually attacked you or anyone whom you know? Or is it all a façade? Test intimidation and see how easily your intimidator's façade crumbles when you challenge it.

Try relaxing and reducing your stress level. Your attacker probably knows just how to get to you mentally and emotionally. Because your attacker has designed careful attacks on your heart and mind, you take these attacks very seriously. They hurt you and trouble you. But if you step back and take a deep breath, you may realize that these attacks are really nothing you need to worry about. Maybe these attacks are based on lies, or maybe they do not matter in the overall scheme of things. Take a day to yourself at the spa or some other relaxing place, far away from the person who is using psychological warfare on you, and think about the attacks and whether or not you are blowing them up in your mind. When you begin to relax and let go of stress, you take back power from your attacker. Things stop bothering you so much and your heart will feel better.

Your heart and your mind are usually the victims in psychological warfare, not your body. If the psychological war-monger really wished you dead, he or she or they would have killed you already. The fact that you are still alive today suggests that either your antagonist does not want to kill you, or else he/she/they cannot get away with killing you. Perhaps he or she does not have the means to get away with murder and is terrified of legal repercussions. You are at least temporarily safe from bodily harm. Do not let your attacker instill fear of death in you.

But time is of the essence. You cannot let your temporary safety give you a false sense of permanent security. Things can quickly change as your antagonist's plan unfolds. You need to take action to protect yourself immediately, in preparation against future physical harm. If someone hates you enough to perform psychological torture upon you, then that person is also capable of murdering you.

Even if you are never physically harmed, mental destruction can be just as disastrous for your life as physical destruction. You may develop a host of mental illnesses in response to the trauma wreaked upon you. You will never be the same. You will deal with self-delusions, hallucinations, depression, and other issues for the rest of your life. Your mind will no longer be your property, but rather the plaything of another person or persons whom you do not know. As you have seen in this book, psychological warfare can take hold of you and transform you into another person. It is insidious and it is effective.

They are taking your life slowly but surely. They may as well kill you, since they are stealing your willpower, your freedom of will, and your will to live. You need to put an end to it before they truly disable you and ruin your life. Take back your power now before more of it is stolen from you.

No one is truly safe. Many of us have been victims of psychological warfare in the past. The media is a possible source of propaganda brainwashing countless people today as we speak.

But you are already ahead of most people in your understanding of psychological warfare. While most people deny its existence, you understand that psychological warfare is real and that it works. You are therefore more prepared to protect yourself. Understanding the problem is one of the first steps to solving the problem.

Protecting Your Loved Ones

You can protect your loved ones by limiting social media and other forms of media. The less that they are exposed to certain media, the less likely they are to be exposed to any propaganda that can affect them adversely.

You can also teach your kids to think for themselves and to respect themselves. Teach them what manipulation looks like and tell them that it is never OK. Teach them to research everything that they hear, even in school, and to always be suspicious of things.

Be frank and open about the reality of psychological warfare with your loved ones.

Provide plenty of real-life examples. This way, your family can become aware of the danger. Awareness can enable them to take steps to fight the problem.

Conclusion

This has been your introduction to psychological warfare, the art of disabling and defeating your enemies mentally. In these pages, you have learned many secret, dark, and powerful tools that enable you to mentally manipulate and harm others. You have learned how to ensure your chances of winning any war, through tried and true psychological methodology.

Now this book has ended, but your foray into the dark science of psychological warfare does not have to. You can continue to employ these methods every day. You can also do more research and become more adept at psychological warfare.

Psychological warfare is hardly a new concept. It has been around for a very long time. Humans have long known that psychology is more powerful and more effective than physical brutality, and so psychological warfare has long been a popular accompaniment to war. It only became a subject of public fascination after World War II. As a result, most people are unaware of psychological warfare.

This is what makes psychological warfare so effective. People will never guess that you are employing these dark tactics on them. It is practically unheard of and certainly misunderstood. Some people even dismiss these concepts as conspiracy nonsense and refuse to believe in the power of psychological warfare. Use their ignorance to your advantage and let them play dumb as you overpower their minds.

What you choose to use this book for is entirely your prerogative. You may use it for harm. You may use it to satisfy simple and plain curiosity about the more hidden concepts of psychology that the mainstream psychology field does not want you to see. You may even use this book to find out how to defend yourself or prepare yourself against future psychological warfare. This book certainly can help you achieve any one of these purposes.

But after reading this book, you will never be the same. The methods outlined in these pages will remain in your head. You may start using them with great success, without even meaning to. Now that you are at the conclusion, you have successfully armed yourself with very deep and skillful psychological warfare tactics that will help you win any battle against any person at any time.

Psychological warfare is hardly a joke or conspiracy theorist conjecture. It is actually used by governments and documented throughout history. Now, in the era of the Internet and Information Age, this form of warfare is even more feasible and effective. You really can ruin lives with psychological warfare and you can reach many more people with propaganda than ever before. Never underestimate the power of psychological warfare or dismiss it as something that cannot possibly do much harm. It really can.

Also never underestimate how suddenly you can become a victim. Always keep your ears and eyes open and take everything with a grain of salt. You should not lie around helpless, waiting for things to get better, if you are under psychological attack. The damage that your mind may sustain from psychological attack is no joke and your life can be permanently destroyed if you do not take action now.

Thank you for reading this. This book is undoubtedly one of the most valuable guides you will have ever read. It has already had a profound effect upon you and will change your life forever. Use it wisely, and watch how suddenly opposition will fall away and the things you want become available to you.

Other great books by Madison Taylor on Kindle, paperback and audio

Rejection Proof Therapy 101: How To Overcome, Deal With And Heal Yourself From Rejection

Cognitive Behavioral Therapy For Beginners: How To Use CBT To Overcome Anxieties, Phobias, Addictions, Depression, Negative Thoughts, And Other Problematic Disorders

Forbidden Psychology 101: The Cool Stuff They Didn't Teach You About In School

Escaping the Introvert World: The Introvert's Guide To Overcoming Shyness, Social Anxiety, And Fear To Thrive In An Extrovert World

NLP For Beginners: Learn the Secrets of Self Mastery, Developing Magnetic Influence and Reaching Your Goals Using Neuro-Linguistic Programming

Depression Proof Yourself: How To Avoid And Overcome Being Depressed

Love Thyself: The First Commandment to Raising your Self Esteem, Boosting your Self-Confidence, and Increasing your Happiness

The Art of Decision Making: How to Make Better Choices in Love, Life, and Work

Sources

The Thirty-Six Strategies. (2016). Easy Strategy. Retrieved from http://www.easy-strategy.com/thirty-six-strategies.html. Based on Sun Tzu's *The Art of War*.

Machiavelli, N. (1513~). *The Prince*.

Made in the USA
Middletown, DE
01 June 2017